Kenerly Presents Publications
P.O. Box 562674
Charlotte, NC 28213

kenerlypresents.com

shauntakenerlypresents@gmail.com

Charlotte, N.C.

First Edition: February 2016

10 9 8 7 6 5 4 3 2 1

Cover Design: Muneca Smith

Printed in the United States of America

<u>*The Right One at the Wrong Time....*</u>

By Anitra Hill

KENERLY PRESENTS PUBLICATION

Chapter 1 The Beginning

In the mean streets of Portsmouth, Virginia was where the players played and the hustler's hustled. These were the same streets that loved no one but everyone seemed to love them. You had to get it how you lived. That was what Lionel "D-Man" Hayes lived by. His loved ones called him Lionel but the streets called him D-Man short for Dope Man. He was a big time hustler and was known from city to city throughout the Tidewater area. He was well loved by all because although he was wealthy, he didn't hesitate to share his wealth with his people that had fallen on hard times.

He supplied other local and new to the game hustlers with work. He paid off the snake cops that wanted a piece of his wealth. They hounded him and his people on the streets until he started to pay them off. He kept a lot of families fed, he looked after the families of loyal hustlers that had gotten knocked off by the feds. He was a good guy and even though he didn't always do right he knew that he was truly blessed and for that reason alone it made it easy for him to help others without looking for anything in return except loyalty. Lionel didn't have the fanciest car because that was one of the true O.G.'s rules, to never flash your accomplishments unless they were obtained legally.

Lionel met and fell in love with one of the local hood stars, the always fly diva that was wanted by many of the hustlers but only taken by the best. Lionel snatched her up quick and changed her name to Martina Hayes. This was very surprising to most because once upon a time he had dedicated his life and his time to the streets. He made

Martina an exception to the rules and he gave her the world and treated her as a true queen. Martina loved the royal treatment that Lionel gave her but often took him for granted. The finest handbags she had them, the fanciest and classiest clothes and jewels- she kept them. Whatever she wanted you best believe he provided her with, but the one thing that he failed to give her was his time. He didn't have all the time in the world for her as she wanted but he made sure that he was in the house each night by 10pm and Sundays were strictly devoted to her. Martina became very unhappy a long time before Lionel noticed her losing interest.

Martina had fallen out of love with him but she loved what he could do for her. She loved the man that he was capable of being, but he was so caught up in the streets that he didn't even realize the change in her. She had begun to stay out until after he would come home and started spending time with friends that he never knew existed. Once shit in the streets had started to get fucked up was when he decided to lay low for a couple of days and then he realized her change.

His main man Zuce had gotten locked up and his right hand man Bamboo was acting shady and Lionel had no idea as to why, so he just assumed that he was having problems with one of his lady friends so he just left it alone. Lionel decided to go home and surprise Martina with flowers, a 14 carat gold tennis bracelet with the necklace to match. He had also booked a hotel for the two of them in a luxury hotel suite in Williamsburg for the week.

When he walked into their 4 bedroom condo he found her sitting at their $1500 8 person kitchen set with the high back leather chairs crying and drinking wine. He rushed over to his wife to embrace her until he noticed a

4

white object in her hand.

"What's wrong Tina, why are you crying? Is it something that I've done?"

After holding her for what seemed like 5 minutes and listening to her sobs he reached for her hands and removed the object which he then realized that it was something that could affect their lives forever.

"Lionel I might as well come out with it and tell you what I've been waiting to tell you for the last 2 months. I'm pregnant Lionel and I've just been scared to find out the obvious. I've been in this house sick and you knew nothing of it, that's how far out there in the streets you are Lionel."

Martina began to cry as she poured her heart out to her husband. Lionel was taken by surprise and promised her that he was going to do right.

"I'm gonna get out the game Tina. Whatever I gotta do to make you and my baby happy. Cry no more baby. Matter of fact pack your bags because I got something planned for us for this week."

After making a phone call to her mystery friend Martina's whole attitude had changed. She went from wanting to be happy that her man had said that he was going to give up the game for her and their unborn baby. To having an attitude as though the person that she was on the phone with gave her an unpleased notion that they were unsatisfied with her.

Lionel not knowing what was on her mind he just took it as if it was just a pregnancy thing. The phone rang again as Martina was about to go and meet her husband at the car so she answered it and the male voice on the other end of the receiver sounded angry.

"You better let him know that this baby isn't his because I'm not seeing another nigga play daddy to my baby. So you better tell him before I do" and hung up without any other words being exchanged.

This let Martina know that her secret was about to come to the light, either voluntarily or involuntarily. Well I might as well make the best of my week before the shit hit the fan she thought. Martina finally pulled herself together as she prepared to head out to the car.

The ride to Williamsburg Resort Hotel and Suites was a quiet one. Both of them were in their own thoughts and for different reasons. Lionel was thinking about how the game had changed right before his very eyes. Niggas went from hustling to feed their families to sticking up the next nigga because he was getting more money than him. They had even started snitching on the next man to save their own asses. Niggas out here playing unfair in the game right now and I care not to be a part of it and plus I got a seed on the way. So I gotta step up and be the man that my wifey needed me to be thought Lionel.

Martina on the other hand had much more going on than anyone even knew anything about. She was either 2 or 3 months pregnant and didn't think that her husband was the father, which lead to her next problem. She had been creeping for the last 4 months and when Lionel finds out she'll have all hell to pay. That's not only because of the fact that she's been creeping but it's the mystery man that she's been creeping with.

Chapter 2 The Get-A-Way

Arriving at the beautiful and luxurious 5-star hotel, the couple eyes were of those that were in total awe because they had been in several hotels all over the world but none this classy. When you pulled up all you would see was the beautiful over-sized chandeliers from the outside and a landscaping view of waterfalls all over the property. A man made pond in the center of the resort with all kinds of colorful fish and huge beautiful unreal looking swans.

As they pulled up to the front sliding doors the valet hurried to greet them before Lionel could even exit the driver's seat and said "Welcome to Williamsburg Resort Hotel and Suites where our pleasure is to please you. May I start by removing your bags and parking your vehicle for you sir?"

After the over friendly valet associate removed all of their luggage from their rented Cadillac they proceeded to the check in counter where the clerk was already ready to service them.

Their check in went just as smooth as well and they were escorted to their presidential suite where they were highly pleased with the selection that was chosen by Lionel. He flashed a grin of pride in himself for doing such a fine job in choosing such a classy spot with the matching suite. Just as he asked for he had a fully stocked bar inside the room and fully stocked kitchen with all the foods that you could think of. A freshly ran hot bath with pink rose petals floating and candles lit around the double occupancy tub and a tray of fresh fruits waiting for them on them on the countertop.

"Wow this is elegant Lionel. You have really outdone yourself this time," said Martina as she met Lionel's embrace and blessed him with a very sensual kiss.

For this was the first form of affection between the two in a matter of weeks. It felt good to be held by one another. They enjoyed one another's kiss for about 5 minutes then Martina began to unbutton Lionel's 8 button Nautica shirt. He grabbed her breasts firmly just as he knew she liked him to.

"Oh my god I haven't felt the sensual touch of my husband in so long and it feels so good," thought Martina.

"These hard nipples between my fingertips feel like butter being glazed on a honey roll." Lionel thought. He said while looking at her honey smooth skin admiring every inch of her curvaceous frame. "Damn I love this woman." Lionel thought.

As Martina began to undress her king he followed her lead by taking off each item of her clothing with a kiss to follow. As he unbuttoned her BCBG blouse he kissed her from her chest down to her once used to be flat stomach. He didn't stop until she was down to her Victoria's Secret bra and panty set and her BCBG pumps. He just stopped to stare at her before he went to devour all of her juices. He began to kiss her thighs while leaving kiss prints trailing down her juicy and hairless vagina. Lionel began to kiss her pussy lips and slid his tongue in and out of her slippery vagina while at the same time exploring it with his 5 fingers. She began to feel a sensation that she had never felt before and she was loving it. She began to moan louder and louder as each of his touches began to weaken her more and more.

Martina began to stroke Lionel's penis in the direction of its built in curve, fast and then slow until Lionel's leg began to shake. She then halted before he would release any of his clear substances. Martina leaned in for another round of his sweet tender kisses and once she felt as if it was safe to take charge of his penis, she takes his manhood into her mouth. With his whole swollen penis in her mouth pulsating, she grabbed his large balls and began to massage them as if she was doing it for relaxation.

Her vagina began to get as wet as her mouth and Lionel loved it. He stuck 2 fingers into her sloppy vagina. Lionel felt himself about to explode so he then pulled her up off his dick and began to play with her. Lionel aroused her breasts once more until her leg quivered and he knew she was about to reach her climax. Feeling as though he had reached a point of inner pride within himself, he then pulled her on top of him as she began to tease his fully grown penis by gently grabbing his penis with her pussy lips and then quickly letting go. This not only excited him but it also sent her into a sense of satisfaction. Once she couldn't take anymore of her own teasing acts of pleasure she went down on her knees once more and began to deepthroat his dick until he grabbed the fresh linens on the king sized bed. Lionel pulled Martina up onto him and planted her goodies right smack dead onto his lips. He began to drink her juices as she took all of him into her mouth as he began to jerk. Normally she would have stopped and allowed him to explore all avenues of her overactive wet pussy until he began to calm himself, but not this time. She allowed him to release himself without hesitation into her mouth. For the first time in their history of love making together she invited him to cum into her mouth without a fight. This not only amazed Lionel but it also turned him on even more because this was the same women that always would pull up and out quickly allowing him to release onto her face and breasts. As Lionel finished dispensing himself into her mouth he took a breath and then scooped her into his arms. He carried her into the bathroom and she climbed into the bathtub that was still warm thanks to the heater function built into the tub. The rose petals began to float as her body hit the water. She felt the flutters in her stomach and all of the joy and excitement that was filled within her quickly turned into sadness. But before the tears filled up into her eyelids could fall Lionel washed them away with her plush wash rag. He washed every inch of her body with her favorite scent Sweet Amber Kisses and Lilac by Victoria's Secret that he had went and picked up for the occasion along with the new robe, nighty and perfume with the teddy bear to match all in her favorite color of pink.

It was funny how when her husband was being her husband and not in the streets. She was so content and happy. As he kissed and washed her he also washed away her troubles as well. After their bath together, she then fed him strawberries with whipped cream and chocolate as he massaged her feet.

An Hour Later

They're back at it again. For some reason Martina couldn't get enough of her husband. After his third vodka and cranberry Martina was at it again. This time she felt the need to stimulate him mentally, so she cut the radio on and started to do a strip tease in her brand new pink teddy. She started to wind her hips to the song "Love you down." This was brand new for Lionel because he was used to his wife being too classy and what some may have called uppity.

"Something has truly gotten into my wife because she is normally just into uniform sex," thought Lionel.

Throwing her BCBG pump over his shoulder and gyrating her hips at the same time took the cake for Lionel because he knew that she definitely learned a few new tricks. He liked it on one hand and was concerned on the other because he was worried that these tricks were practiced on someone else before him and whomever that someone else was had truly brought the freak out of her. He didn't know whether to be upset or to be ashamed that he had neglected his wife that bad that she had to go elsewhere?

"Is there someone else? Fuck it!" Lionel thought.

"What's in the past is the past, it's my fault anyways because I should have been doing my job and pleasing my wife" Lionel thought while shaking his head.

Martina noticed Lionel spaced out. She bought him back to reality with the removing of her nighty and massaging her own breasts with enjoyment. He began to rub her legs and licking his lips like he could taste her on his tongue. She then went over to the bar and dipped one of the strawberries into the whipped cream and began to tease him with it with her tongue. Martina placed two cherries into the whipped cream and sat them on both of her nipples as he began to eat them off and playing with her clitoris at the same time. This time he took his time with her and with every stroke he talked dirty to her. He told her how he had neglected her for so long and how it was all an eye opener and it's all a lot clearer now. The dirty words mixed with the idea of her husband knowing the truth filled her with confusion and that started to take over her mind. At that moment the words that Lionel began to say to her sounded foreign.

"Martina I love you with all of me and I know that you love me just as well. I want to put the past in the past and let you know that I forgive you just as I hope that you forgive me for neglecting you." As Lionel looked at Martina with tears in his eyes he noticed her crying even harder.

Martina stopped him mid-stroke and said to him "Lionel I have a secret to tell you and I can't live with it any longer."

Lionel stopped her before she could say anymore. He said in a sincere tone, "Tina let it be just that. A secret. A secret that you will take to your grave because in my heart I've already forgiven you for any wrong that you may have done. I love you and I mean that unconditionally."

At that point Martina realized why she had fallen in love with Lionel because of the kind of heart that he was blessed with.

They enjoyed the week in Williamsburg with plenty of off the wall sex, shopping and adventures like museums, art galleries, historic galleries and walks in the park. They just enjoyed life and getting to know one another all over again and they talked about their future together raising their baby.

On their last night at the resort, Lionel had one last surprise for Martina. As they walked back into their room from a day of shopping, they were greeted by a professional chef with platters set up along the countertop with finger foods such as shrimp, chicken wings, meatballs, kabobs and much more. Lionel walked Martina to the candle lit table set for two and as he pushed her chair up under her, he presented her with a box. He got down on one knee and asked her if she would accept this new wedding ring as a start to a new beginning. With tears in her eyes she happily accepted with gratefulness.

In his eyes whatever secret Martina was holding in he cared to hear nothing about. This was what they were calling their new beginning. Although he couldn't decide whether he didn't want to hear the truth because of being afraid of not being able to trust her again or was it because he just couldn't handle the truth?

Six Months Later

Their new beginning was going great. The couple had fallen back in love and was simply loving life with one another again. Lionel made a positive change in his life like he had promised his wife that he would.

Once they had returned back from their getaway, Lionel met with all those that were a part of his team. He let them know that he had a change of heart and that he was giving up the streets.

"Fella's I've called you all here today to let you all know firsthand that I'm giving all this shit up. Shit gets old and I'm tired of looking over my shoulder and not being able to really enjoy my life. Besides all of that I have a seed on the way," said Lionel with pride.

"Need not say anymore D-Man. I commend you for doing the right thing because I know a lot of cats out here that wouldn't or should I say couldn't just walk away from the streets just like that. With all this money out here, that just goes to show you that you're not a greedy nigga. You've done a lot for people out here in these streets and I thank you for it all," said his right hand man Bamboo.

For the next 3 days after that D-Man Hayes went around collecting the last of his dirty money off the streets from his people that owed him money to add to his stash. In which was a pretty penny that he was sitting on. No one knew anything about his stash and that's how he felt that it should be. Real G's move in silence he always said. That was that, he had gotten his money from everyone except one surprising person.

One of the people that he did the most for out here, Bamboo. Bamboo was very anxious for D-Man to give it all up but refused to pay him what he owed him. Bamboo owed D-Man Hayes $15,000 and every time D-Man asked him about his money over the past couple of days Bamboo would brush him off making all kinds of lame excuses.

"I gotta go get it out of the bank."

"I'm waiting on ole boy to pay me."

Now come on now does that nigga think I'm a damn fool cause any nigga that hustle knows that you're not putting that type of bread into the bank, if you're hustling and don't have a job to back it up, thought D-Man. Then he told him that somebody owed him some money and he was waiting on his peoples to pay him what he owed him and that he was gonna give it to him then. Then the final excuse was that his lady was pregnant and he couldn't afford to give it all to him right then. D-Man had to think long and hard about that thing and wasn't sure of what he thought about it. He was kind of puzzled because he knew that Bamboo had lady friends and most of them he knew but when he asked him which one it was that was knocked, he would dodge the question.

"Oh you don't know her, this one is an exclusive

one."

Bamboo would never even as much as give a name of this exclusive young lady. Leaving the situation alone because he knew that Bamboo had been acting shady lately but he couldn't figure out why his right hand man was going against the code of the streets. That was to never leave an open debt, in other words when a nigga basically putting food in your mouth that you don't bite the hand that feed you. D-Man Hayes was a stand-up type of dude and just letting it go as a loss.

A couple of months later, all the dudes that hustled with D-Man looked out and got together and threw him a party celebrating his decision to give up the game. They also made it like a baby shower for the couple where they collected money for their new baby girl that would be arriving any day. Martina was a little skeptical about going to the party but Lionel refused to let her stay home alone. He knew that she could go into labor at any time. She had no choice but to go to the party.

Martina looked beautiful as ever with her soft yellow Kira Roberts designer dress and her silver peep toe heels. She wore her long flowing hair in a pin-up. Her jewelry and makeup to accented the whole attire. Lionel had on the matching Dekion Davinci suit that complimented Martina's dress very well. The suit fit perfect on Lionel's broad shoulders and Martina's eyes had a glow in them when she saw her husband in his ensemble.

This was really one of Martina's first outings. Their new beginning. She had changed her number and cut all ties with old friends except for her best friend Terri. If she would go anywhere it was with Terri and they would mainly go shopping or out to eat. They would never shop in

Portsmouth. They always shopped either in Virginia Beach, Williamsburg or the Richmond area.

When Lionel and Martina had arrived at the private club called 'Images' they noticed the parking lot was filled to the max. Walking inside it looked like a tasteful player's ball because everybody was dressed up like the players. They did a wonderful job with putting the whole thing together, it was decorated lovely. It was great to see so many people come together for the occasion. The food was catered by "The Porters," they had a chain of restaurants around the seven cities and their food was top chef material. They had DJ Pernell spinning the records and also had an open bar in which everyone was taking advantage of except Martina and Lionel. Everything was going good up until Bamboo got drunk...

Chapter 3 Doing A Bid

At the Portsmouth Federal Prison sat Zuce in an angry rage because of the fucked up shit that he had just heard that's been going down in the streets with his long term running partners Bamboo and D-Man. It's funny how news travel in the jails and prisons faster than on the streets to the streets.

"Oh hell naw, this nigga is just breaking all kinds of rules of the hustle. You never cross your peoples we have always said and this nigga goes and fucks this man's wife and is possibly the father of the baby that she is carrying. Hell no!" Zuce said to himself. "I gotta call and see what's up with this shady ass nigga."

Back At The Party

Mario who was one of the youngest hustlers on the block goes around to collect the money from the other guests for their baby girl, which was a tradition of theirs. Instead of buying gifts they collected the dough and gave it to the couple. As Martina and D-Man sat and mingled with the others D-Man noticed the evil stares that Bamboo was sending his way. D-Man just brushed it off and took it as he was just drunk and had a lot on his mind. Just then an old school friend of D-Man's that came back in town came over to the table to holler at D-Man. After D-Man introduced his friend Tim to his wife she excused herself to go to the ladies room. As Martina was walking to the restroom she didn't even notice Bamboo watching her every move.

Locked away in the bathroom Martina felt safe because the whole night she's felt uncomfortable because of the one reason she didn't want to attend the party --her mystery man-- Bamboo and he looked as if he no longer wanted it to be a mystery. She no longer had any communication with Bamboo. Since the Get-a-Way she looked at it as she had fun while it lasted --Regretted it-- so she left it alone for the sake of them both. She changed her number because he would call and call her over and over again. He would leave all sorts of threatening messages and confessions of his love messages as well, each and every day. She just got tired of it and felt that she should just change her number to cut all communication between the two of them.

While standing in the bathroom she felt an uneasy feeling in her stomach and wasn't sure if it was contractions or just her nerves playing tricks on her. So she thought maybe it was just her nerves. She just brushed it off and went to the sink to check her face and fix her clothes before walking out the bathroom door. Walking out the door at that particular time was a huge mistake because Bamboo was right outside the door waiting, as soon as she walked out the door. Bamboo pushed her back in and locked it.

"You fucking selfish bitch! Oh so you thought that you could just change your fucking number on me and leave me and that just be that?" Bamboo shouted.

He had her pinned up against the stall with his hand against her neck and his nose in her hair, smelling it like it turned him on.

"Get the fuck off of me Marcus (which was Bamboo's real name). We had our fun but now it's over so just leave me alone." Martina said calmly because she just knew that he wouldn't hurt her, at least that's what she thought anyways.

As he begun to stare at her with lust in his eyes, she tried to remove herself from his unwanted embrace but that just pissed him off even more because she was no longer under his spell to do whatever it was that he wanted of her. That was to remain his freak.

With a tap on the door and concern in his heart for his wife he was in rage because Mario had just came to him and told him to come check on his wife. Mario had seen Bamboo waiting by the ladies room door and then pushed Martina back in when she was coming out. As D-Man listened with his ear to the door he could hear his wife's cries.

"Please just get off of me and let me go, you're hurting me."

D-Man kicked the plywood door in just as Bamboo was about to rape his wife. D-Man went charging at Bamboo and Martina cried tears of HELP!!!!! As the two men wrestled D-Man of course got the best of Bamboo because of his slow reflexes due to the alcohol. D-Man decided not to take it to him as he knew that he could. But with all of his concentration focused on Bamboo he didn't even notice his wife in the corner balled up in a knot in pain until Shayla in which was Mario's girlfriend came in to check on Mrs. Martina as she always called her. Mario always called her Aunt Martina and Uncle D-Man because of their close relationship, Mario was Bamboo's son but D-Man practically raised him and taught him about being a man.

"Mr. D-Man we have to get Mrs. Martina to the hospital very soon."

Without hesitation D-Man snapped back to reality and jumped off of Bamboo. He turned to Shayla and Martina's direction and then D-Man went to tend to his wife. With tears in her eyes because of what her husband just had to witness. Lionel scooped his wife up in his arms to take her to the hospital, with Mario and Shayla right there by their side.

When they arrived at Maryview Medical Center, Lionel threw the car in park and jumped out to get a wheelchair for his wife who was now in so much more pain. As Lionel was pushing Martina away in the wheelchair he made sure that he told his wife how much he loved her and that he was going to be there for her the whole step of the way. Mario jumped into the driver's seat of D-Man's car and parked it properly. He and Shayla then rushed into the hospital to meet up with Lionel and Martina. As they entered the Emergency room, Lionel's cell phone began to ring and he just handed it to Mario for him to take the call. It was a collect call from Zuce at the prison. Mario accepted the call and Zuce was in a rage yelling and shouting into the receiver.

"Yo who is this!? Is this you nephew?"

"Yes Uncle Zuce this is me."

Zuce then kept on with his rage and asked, "Yo nephew did you tell your uncle what you told me about your pops?"

"Naw Unc I haven't had a chance to tell em yet because of everything that has been going on lately. But that shit hit the fan tonight at the party Unc. Uncle D-Man fucked my pops up and his ass deserved it too. The whole night pops had been staring at Aunt Martina and was gritting on Uncle D-Man. When Aunt Martina got up to go to the bathroom my pops followed her and nobody noticed it but me. I was collecting the money for the baby when I saw him plotting. I then told Shayla to collect the rest of the money and I then went and got Uncle D-Man when I saw my pops push Aunt Martina back into the bathroom when she was coming out. So I told Uncle D-Man what I saw and him and I went to the bathroom and Uncle D-Man heard her crying for my pops to get off of her. Uncle D-Man just snapped and kicked the door off of the hinges. He saw pops about to rape her, so now we're at the hospital because auntie was in a whole lot of pain." Mario testified.

After a couple of seconds of silence Zuce told him, "Nephew I swear to god I know that is your pops and I thank you for standing up and doing the noble thing by telling me the 411 out there on the streets. But he has to be dealt with and I have no problem with calling my proper authorities to handle the job."

Mario then replied by saying, "Unc I feel you and Uncle D-Man have been more of a father figure to me and then my pops has ever have. Or ever could been. If you ask me he's dead in my eyes and if you need me to handle it I will cause he not only shitted on me as a child but he also broke the code of the streets and betrayed family. That's a No-No."

As Mario was on the phone he paced the Maryview Medical Hospital floor with sincere hate in his eyes. "Naw nephew I got this. You just keep on being there by your uncle's side because he's gonna need you once all this comes out. Make sure that your aunt and the baby are doing ok and that they never want for anything. Lastly make sure that you let your uncle know the whole truth about the situation at hand."

Zuce spoke with sincerity in his voice and it was felt by Mario. At that time their call was over and the phone disconnected. Mario sat there in a trance until Shayla ran up to him with a distraught look on her face and began to cry as she blurted out all sorts of horrible things.

"Aunt Martina's baby died!" Shayla began to cry uncontrollably.

"What happened Shay?" Mario asked frantically.

"I'm not sure Mario as soon as I heard the doctor say that he had good news and some bad news. The bad news was that during all of the drama that Martina had experienced lately the baby was feeding off of Martina's stress and the baby passed away. Then I just ran out of the room to come find you." Shayla said between cries.

"Oh shit, oh shit, oh shit!" Mario shouted as he paced the floor. "So I wonder what the good news was then." Mario thought.

Inside of the Labor and Delivery after the death of baby girl Promise

Inside of the 'Labor and Delivery' waiting area awaited lovers Shayla and Mario concerned for their role models Martina and Lionel. They had been waiting out there for a little over an hour to hear about the status of Martina. Hoping for no more bad news. Mario had begun to blame himself for letting this go on for too long and not telling his Uncle D-Man right away but he was just waiting for the right time. Then he realized that no time would ever be the right time to tell your Uncle (that you love and respected) that your pops (that you hated and had no respect for) had been sleeping with his wife for months now. That would do 2 things; hurt a man's pride and get somebody put in the dirt. As Mario began to ponder in his own thoughts, his Uncle D-Man walked into the waiting area with a pair of green scrubs on as if he had just performed surgery himself. Both Shayla and Mario jumped up at the same time to run and join D-Man's embrace. D-Man asked them to sit down because he wanted to talk to them both. This was surprising to Mario because anytime D-Man talked to him about family business he always done it in private and never in front of Shayla.

"Shayla I asked you to stay in on the conversation today because you've proven yourself to be a stand-up chick and you've been there for my nephew even when he's had some fuck-ups. You stood by his side and tonight at the party I saw something that only a true hustler would have seen. You can really be trusted. My nephew has always been taught to not trust just anyone, learn them first by sitting back and observing and that is exactly what he does. He does not trust easily but he did tonight. He left it in your hands to collect our money for our baby girl from everyone and that says a lot. You done just that and done it with pride. So Miss Shayla you are now an official part of my family." D-Man said with a big grin on his face to Shayla as Shayla and Mario sat with big Kool-Aid grins on their faces.

"Now for you Mario, I am so proud to see the man that I've taught you to be. You should have been my son because all your daddy did was make you. Ha ha ha ha naw but thank you for coming to get me when my wife was in danger. I love my wife and will die for her as well, and that's why I want you to treat this young lady with the most upmost respect. Don't do like me and put the streets first and push her into the arms of another man cause that's what I did nephew. I pushed your aunt into the arms of your pops and as much as I wanna be mad at them I can't because if I would have been there for my wife then she wouldn't have ever cheated on me. She got tired and she tried to tell me time and time again that she was lonely but all I did was chase that paper. GREED, greed nephew will get you fucked up in more ways than one. So keep this gem on your arm and don't let her go because she reminds me of your aunt Tina when we were growing up." D-Man said with tears in his eyes.

"Unc I wanted to tell you so many times but I just couldn't bring myself to tell you something that would hurt you. If you want me to I will dead em for you. Cause he means nothing to me. You're my real dad. That nigga is just taking up space on this earth." Mario said with anger in his raspy voice. Shayla sat in tears as she had mixed emotions about what she was hearing because this was the first time that she'd heard any of this.

"Nephew pump your breaks cause that's one thing that you don't do is wish death upon a man cause you're not God. He will deal with him in due time cause God don't like ugly and if you try to handle it then the Lord can't do his job. Trust me the Lord's work is far more powerful than anything we could ever put on him. So pray on that built up anger that you have in your heart for that no good nigga. You can't live your life to the fullest with all of that hatred in your heart. Now lastly your aunt tried to tell me about your pops affair when we had our Get-A-Way. I made her promise me that she'd keep it a secret because in my eyes she was forgiven as long as she forgave me for not being there for her and we started a new beginning leaving the past in the past. The only reason she told me today was because she felt that she owed me an explanation as to why Bamboo did what he did tonight. Your aunt is doing ok and I'm sure that Shayla told you that because of the stress and the commotion tonight that we lost Baby Promise. That was her name but a blessing came out of it as well. We didn't know that she was pregnant with twins, we just thought that the baby was big. The doctor didn't even see that there was another baby in there. She was hiding and the doctor just thought that the baby had a very strong heartbeat but it was 2 heartbeats that we were hearing all along." D-Man said with a sense of relief in his voice.

"So yall come on in and meet your new baby cousin and your Aunt Martina wants to ask you something Mario."

As they entered the brightly lit labor and delivery room they saw a newborn baby girl with a face of pure beauty and a head full of curly hair just laying so peacefully without a care in the world.

"Come on in y'all and meet Miss Secret Hayes. Look at my baby lying here like a big girl, she's lying here on my chest so peacefully." Tina says looking down a Secret with a smile.

"Thank you Shayla for looking out for a sister cause these brothers here would have just let me die." Martina said with a chuckle, and then the rest of them followed with laughter as well.

"Mario I want to thank you as well for sending me help even though I was wrong. I love you for that."

Martina said as she blew Mario a kiss in the air. "I have something to ask you that's serious and this action will only take place with your approval. You know I was wrong for stepping out on Lionel with Marcus (Bamboo) but I've tried to stop it for months but he blackmailed me. He told me that he was going to tell Lionel a whole bunch of lies and I let my fear took control of me and that wouldn't have been the first time that Marcus would have taken sex from me. He has actually raped me several times." Martina said with tears in her eyes as scenes replayed in her mind of the encounters.

"He would show up at places that I would go and tell me to get into his car and if I would say no then he would threaten me and say that he'd kill Lionel or would kill me or even Mario. He's even said that he'd snitch on Lionel cause he knew everything about his drug business. He'd hold me down and tell me that he'd turn my world upside down." Silence filled the room as everyone sat there in shock because it was everyone's first time hearing the whole truth, even Lionel's. As she continued to talk secret begun to cry and Martina handed her to Shayla for her to hold and then she wiped the tears from her eyes as she continued. "I remember one night that Terri and I went to the Broadway Night Club to have drinks and when we were leaving we went our separate ways and as I was walking to my car I noticed that I had a flat tire. I went into my purse to call Terri to catch a ride with her and Marcus popped up out of nowhere. He said that he'd give me a ride home or asked me if I wanted him to change my tire. I said that I'd like if he'd change my tire and then he just got angry at me.

"Well then it's gonna cost you" I then told him that I'd just call Lionel and he just flipped out and said "Fuck you BITCH call your little bitch ass puppy dog of a husband Lionel. and by the way stop calling him that his name is D-Man". As I was still in his car he yanked at my dress and tore the bottom of it. I reached for the door handle as I was about to get out of his car. He tried to back his car up and apologize but I jumped up and ran back inside of the club and called you Lionel. And when you came and got me I lied to you and told you that I got into a fight with a female in the club and she flattened my tire. I believe in my heart that it was him all along that flattened my tire. The morale of the story is that he has had me under his little black male spell a little too long now and I should have been told you a long time ago Lionel. But I was too afraid to." She then turned to Mario and looked at him with a serious look on her face.

"Mario I know that's your father but I wanna know if you'd be upset with me if I pressed charges on him, because he's not going to stop. I tried to tell myself that he has never hurt me but I was just in denial and trying to give him the benefit of the doubt. I can't jeopardize my family any longer."

Mario was in shock and told her, "Aunt Martina I'm so sorry that you had to go through all of this behind a no good worthless ass nigga. Please excuse my language auntie. You have been the only mother figure that I've had in my life and Uncle D-Man and Uncle Zuce have been the only male figures in my life so to know that he's hurt you repeatedly hurts me inside. So you don't need my approval because since my mom died yall have been my parents so with that being said do what you gotta do. Do it without any hesitation. Now if yall don't mind I'd like to get over here to hold my baby sister, mom and dad." Mario said with a Kool-Aid grin on his face talking to Lionel and Martina as they looked proud.

2 hours later and the family still sit in the hospital room enjoying one another and Shayla attached to baby Secret. Mario and Lionel decided to go out and get something to eat from the cafeteria downstairs. The two

ladies sat and watched BET as Martina fed Baby Secret and the door opened. The smell of alcohol ran through the room way before the face appeared in the room. Bamboo walked in drunk as ever. As he staggered in, Shayla stood up and walked over to the bed to be beside Martina.

"Well, well, well, looka here. My baby girl is finally here" Bamboo slurred his words.

While Bamboo was talking to Martina, Shayla begun texting Mario, telling him that they needed to get up there fast because Bamboo was up there drunk. Bamboo then proceeded to talk and stare at Martina with a crazed look.

"Let me hold my baby girl Tina. Damn I sure do make some pretty babies don't I Shayla. "You should know because my son got you whipped."

Shayla sat without saying a word and this only made Bamboo mad. Then he said with frustration in his voice "Look you little bitch I know you hear me talking to you! My son got you trained well don't he bitch!"

He went to grab for Baby Secret, Shayla begun to chant "Devil I rebuke you in the name of Jesus! Devil I rebuke you in the name of JESUS!" Shayla said with her finger pointed in Bamboo's face. She pointed with authority and as soon as she said it a second time Lionel and Mario came busting into the room. Bamboo looked startled and cheap in the face.

"What's up D-Man, what's up son. You see your little sister?"

Mario shot back "Naw bitch you didn't have nothing to do with this one and this is my little sister but only because D-Man is my real Pops. You're just a piece of shit and the next time that you disrespect my mom's over there or my lady, nobody will be able to save your ass. And trust me I do mean no one."

D-man sat with his hands balled up inside of one another and then walked closer to Bamboo looking at him like he should feel threatened.

"Nigga you've been my brother since middle school. You go and fuck me over like this. You've always wanted to be me anyways so I don't know why I'm surprised." D-Man chuckled and continued to say "But nigga fucking my wife don't and won't MAKE YOU ME NIGGA. Then you try some hoe shit and rape her what that tell you nigga. You're nowhere. You can never be me or nothing like me because for one YOU'RE STRAIGHT BITCH! I should straight merck your bitch ass now but I told my nephew oops I meant MY SON nigga, yeah I said my son because all you did was help make him my nigga. I told my son not to deal with you so I'm not going to deal with you. I'm gonna let the Lord deal with you but if you come anywhere near my wife, my kids or my daughter-in-law ever again I PROMISE YOU - WORD ON MY DEAD DAUGHTER PROMISE, I SWEAR I WONT BE ABLE TO WAIT ON THE LORD TO DEAL WITH YOU BECAUSE YOU WILL BE DEAD IN 2.2 SECONDS! TRUST ME ON THAT ONE NIGGA." Lionel finished, then there was a knock on the door.

Three Portsmouth Police entered and Bamboo looked stupid and scared as hell in the face. The officers said that they are here for a disturbance.

"Yes officers, this gentleman here that is smelling of alcohol tried to rape me earlier and fought me. He caused me to lose my twin baby girl Promise and now he's up here putting his hands on me again. He is threatening each of us in this room sir." Martina said with a sigh.

The officer cut her off and said, "Ma'am did you just say that because this gentleman put his hands on you earlier today, that has caused you to lose your twin baby girl?"

"Yes sir I did." Martina answered in a shaky tone.

"Were you guys there when this happened?"

Everyone nodded in agreement and the Chinese Jackie Chan looking officer said "Let me go out to the front desk and get some medical records." Bamboo stood with a stupid look on his face.

"Officer these are all lies. See look there's my baby girl right there." He said and pointing to Baby Secret.

As the two officers questioned everyone and took their statements the third officer came back into the room with a handful of papers and told Bamboo "Sir you're under arrest for being drunk in public, and if this young lady here would like to press charges I can run down a list of other charges to you. Ma'am would you like to press charges?" Martina nodded her head yes and the three officers hauled Marcus "Bamboo" Leight off to jail.

Chapter 4 A Trip To Jail And Day In Court

The ride downtown was a long ride for Bamboo as he sat in the back of the too tight police cab crying and wondering how his life turned out to be so ugly so fast. First my wife Debbie died on me when my baby boy was only 2 years old. Now he's 18 and to make matters worse he hates the ground that I walk on. The closest thing that I had to family was D-Man and he wanted to kill me and hell I can't say that I blame him cause I was wrong. Shit I violated him. Since we were in the 6th grade D-Man had it all. The looks, the gear, cars and all the girls wanted him and he had the baddest chick ever in my eyes Martina. I saw Martina first when we were in high school but she dissed me and come to find out it was for that nigga Lionel. Just like that he had her but I always told myself that I was going to get her and when we got older I saw my opportunity and I took it. She was lonely because this nigga was busy in these streets hustling. I offered to take her and her best friend Terri out and they accepted. I paid for everything including all of their drinks and got them pissy drunk. I finally got what I wanted, my best friend, my brother's wife. I had her in the palm of my hand, but I did what D-Man always said was the #1 rule on the streets "DON'T GET TOO GREEDY." Greed would get you fucked up in more ways than one. I chuckled hearing D-Man in his head telling him that.

"I got greedy and it cost me everything." Said Bamboo regretfully to the officer that was transporting him to the Regional jail.

"So do you really think that this baby is yours?"

The nosey officer asked, interested because his life had no action like any of this.

"Naw I know it isn't because the doctors told me a long time ago that I couldn't produce kids. Mario isn't even mine but my wife was pregnant when I got with her and I just told everybody that he was mine. What made it worse was that I thought that Mario was D-Man's son but he didn't even know it. When him and I were out in these streets hard, we were at this strip club called Majik City and we both bet on which one could get Debbie first and he got her that night and I fucked around and wifed her."

"So Mr. Leight you mean to tell me that this could be Lionel's son and he doesn't even know?" The officer inquired amazed.

"Nope because I never brought Debbie around. I moved her out of Portsmouth and moved her or shall I say us to Virginia Beach. No one ever knew it because the code of the streets was to never turn a hoe into a housewife. Once again I went against the code and fell in love with her too. She was a good woman. She was special and no one would have saw her as that. They would always only see her as a stripper that sometimes turned tricks for extra money. Really she was stripping to pay for school. She wanted to be a nurse and she had 6 more months of RN School left when she died of a heart attack and left me here. ALONE!"

"Well you had your son, why didn't you try to even bond with him?" The officer asked?"

Bamboo paused and then said, "Because every time I looked at that lil dude I saw D-Man and I couldn't take it. That's when I realized that deep down inside that I loved my brother Lionel but I hated D-Man cause he had it all. Everything that I've always wanted." I shocked myself for finally admitting his hatred for my close friend.

As much as the officer hated to end the conversation because his life was far way boring but he had a job to do. Although he kinda felt bad for me he felt for Martina and D-Man way more, so he did his duty and took me to get my mugshot taken and fingerprints. Before the officer walked away I turned to him and looked at him feeling like I had just released a ton of bricks off of my shoulders.

"Thanks for listening to me man and not judging me. Can you please tell D-Man about Mario?

The officer agreed on letting D-Man know about the possibility of fathering a son that he knew nothing of. The officer enjoyed hearing all of the juicy gossip, but he felt sorry for a man that he didn't even know. D-Man!

4 days later in the packed courthouse sat Lionel, Martina and Mario waiting to hear the news on Bamboo's case. Shayla stayed at home with Baby Secret while they all went to court. Marcus "Bamboo" Leight entered the courtroom with shackles on his feet and hands. He looked over at the three people that he had hurt in three different ways but was once close to and put his head down in disgust at himself.

Where they all thought that they'd be satisfied to hear the verdict rule in the favor of them. They were all saddened in their own little ways to hear the last two charges of two counts of attempted murder and one for First Degree Murder and a host of other charges. As they got up to leave the courtroom Bamboo pleaded.

"PLEASE forgive me family. Although I know that doesn't make what I've done to each of you right, I still wanted to say that I'm sorry for the pain that I've caused each of you." Tears fell upon his face as he expressed his sorrow.

And just as quick as it was said from Bamboo, D-Man forgave him and prayed for mercy on his soul as he was sentenced to 69 years in prison. Although Zuce was in jail eating up time behind Bamboo he had no mercy on him because he felt as if he had no loyalty to no one. Zuce and Bamboo ran into one another before Bamboo was to be transferred further in Virginia and Zuce told Bamboo that he was going to get his one way or another. Jail was way too easy for him.

2 days later Bamboo had written a letter to the review board telling them that Zuce Rogers was innocent and that the drugs that they found weren't his. Bamboo lead them to his very own stash house out Virginia Beach to prove to them that he was telling the truth. He also wrote a letter to Zuce, Martina, Lionel and Mario confessing all of his wrong doings amongst each of them and that Zuce was right that he didn't deserve to live and that this was his final goodbye to each of them.

Zuce was released from prison after doing a 6 month bid for something that didn't belong to him but he was planning on just eating the 5 years in prison instead of snitching. Zuce was released because of new evidence that they had gotten from Marcus and that very same day Marcus "Bamboo" Leight was found dead in his cell. He had hung himself once he made sure that Zuce was set free.

This was sad news to everyone in the streets because even though he had done wrong they all forgave him and actually felt sorry for him because he really needed help. He had been going through a state of depression for some time and no one ever knew it. On the day that they found Bamboo dead, the officer from the hospital came to Lionel and Martina's house to speak to Lionel. After telling Lionel about Bamboo's death was when he released the information that Bamboo shared with him the night of the arrest in the back of the police car. He shared all of it and it was funny but it made Lionel miss his friend. It also explained a whole lot of their past. Lionel thanked the officer and went inside to share this with his wife just to see how she'd cope with it. Martina was shocked at the news about Mario and deeply saddened all over again about the news of Marcus "Bamboo." She went into a state of depression of her own because she felt as if she was to blame for his death because she pressed charges on him.

The next day Lionel called Mario and Shayla over to the house to share this information with them and asked Mario if he wanted to do a blood test. Of course he said "No!" Mario said he knew who his father was without it. Lionel then asked Martina if she wanted to get a blood test for Secret and Martina surprisingly said "Yes, just so that later on down the line there would be no questions."

Monday morning came and Lionel took Secret and Mario to both get a blood test done even though it wouldn't change the way that he felt about either of them. As time went past Secret was beginning to look more and more like Mario and Mario had already looked like Lionel but they thought that it was just because they'd been around each other for so long.

Two weeks later the paternity test came back and they were sent to their house and Lionel called Mario over so they could all open it together. When Shayla and Mario arrived they noticed a difference in Martina that Lionel had seen as well. The test determined that Lionel was the father of 18 year old Mario Leight and 1 month old Secret Hayes. Joy filled each of their hearts to finally know the truth but Martina on the other hand looked as if it had made her sad to hear it because she just burst into tears and ran out of the house. For some strange reason Martina was hoping that Secret was Bamboo's so she could still have a piece of him left here on earth with her. She was confused and felt as if she had no one to turn to in her time of need. She felt lost and lonely in this big ole' world and didn't know which way to turn. She then decided to drive down to the waterfront and sit in her favorite spot.

The next morning Martina woke up in her car still parked in the same spot at the waterfront with a banging headache. She pulled out her cell phone and saw that it said 26 missed calls and all of them from Lionel, Shayla and Mario. She thought about how she got out there and she also then wondered how her life had gotten to this point. Her phone began to ring once more and she saw that it was Mario and she decided to answer this time.

"Hello son (attempting to sound calm and normal). Yes, I'm ok. Yes, I slept out here at the waterfront but yes I'm ok. Yes, come on down here and pick me up. Thank you baby"

Martina hung up the phone and tears of sadness and hurt rushed down her face. When Mario and Shayla pulled up, Mario gotten into Martina's car and held her while she cried. Seeing Martina like this really touched him so he just stared at her in awe.

"Ma are you crying because of my test result? Did you not want Pops to be my real dad?"

Martina wiped her tears away with the palm of her hands and then wiped her hands to her shirt to dry them. She turned to him and held his face and chose her words wisely.

"Mario you were already our son before the paternity test came about, so don't you ever think that."

"So what's wrong then Ma? You should be the happy with life right now" Mario asked her trying to find clarity.

"Yeah I should be but I just feel like a piece of me is missing. I feel like I have no purpose here on earth anymore. Yall don't need me. I feel worthless." Martina said rambling on.

Mario sat with his hands up to his face in disbelief of what he had just heard and thought to himself "How can she possibly think that we could make it without her? A few tears fell from Mario's face and Martina patted him on the back and they shared one last embrace. Mario drove Martina's car as Shayla followed behind them in Mario's car.

Mario and Martina rode in silence while each of them waddled in their own thoughts. Every now and then Mario would reach over and grab his mother's hand just to let her know that he was thinking of her at that very moment. Pulling into their driveway seemed like a moment that Martina dreaded, because she had to face her husband and her newborn daughter whom she had just neglected for a whole 24 hours without even giving it a second thought.

Entering their home seemed like it was the wrong thing to do thought Martina.

"How can I possibly come in here and live like nothing has happened. My husband is too good of a man for me. He deserves so much better and my daughter just reminds me of too many memories of the past. I can't possibly live my life like this." Martina said out loud as Lionel walked into the room and heard her say this.

Lionel just hugged his wife as he tried to understand how his wife can just give up on life like this. Martina was really in a deep depression and Lionel worried that she would really try to harm herself and possibly the baby. He just couldn't take that chance. As Lionel hugged Martina he could feel her body shaking and then realized that she was crying silent tears.

"What's wrong Tina?"

She just sits there in a trance in silently.

"Tina, Tina are you ok?"

And then she just started to shout in a loud tone with anger and attitude in her voice, looking like the exorcist. It was as if she was a whole different person, and Lionel didn't like it.

"NO LIONEL IM NOT OK! IT'S ALL YOUR FAULT! IT'S YOUR FAULT THAT I CHEATED! IT'S YOUR FAULT THAT I HAD A BABY THAT I DON'T WANT AND IT'S YOUR FAULT THAT MARCUS IS DEAD! IT'S ALL YOUR FUCKING FAULT!"

Those last words cut Lionel like a knife and he was very hurt and upset that Martina would say a thing like that. He started to spaz out on her but he thought that it be best that he handled her differently.

"I think that's it's best that you go and spend some time away from the house so you can get yourself together." Lionel told her with a stern tone.

Martina just sat there with tears streaming down her face from her eye lids and without second thought she packed her some clothes and left her devoted husband and precious newborn daughter and didn't look back.

Chapter 5 Daddy Dearest 2 ½ Years Later

2 years had went past and Lionel was still raising Secret alone. He had finally talked Mario into joining the Air Force to better himself. Mario and Shayla were still together and doing great. They ended up moving in with Lionel and Secret to help Lionel out since Martina had left them. Lionel really knew nothing about raising a newborn baby but quickly had to learn. On the day that Mario had gotten sworn in they found out that Shayla was 7 weeks pregnant. Mario then knew that he had done the right thing by joining the military. He felt that he owed it to his father to make something of himself and the streets wasn't going to get him anywhere, and on top of all that he had a seed on the way.

Lionel was now an electrician at the Norfolk Naval Shipyard and making a nice amount of money and he was now making it legally. Lionel had never thought that he'd ever see himself working a 9-5 but he knew he had to do whatever he had to do for his family. Shayla was a very big help because she played a big part in helping with the raising of Secret, and Mario loved her even more for that.

Martina was out in the streets more than ever and didn't seem to miss Lionel or her children. She moved in with her best friend Terri for a while until Terri started to nag her about going back home to her family. She then decided to pack up her things and begun to sleep in her car or at different people's houses until she finally got an apartment out the projects. Terri kept Lionel informed on Martina's whereabouts and she would often come over Lionel's house too see Baby Secret and would buy her pampers and clothes. Terri would often tell Lionel that she was sorry for the way that things had turned out with him and Martina. She also told him that she didn't understand why Martina was acting the way that she was acting. When it came to the Martina subject Lionel felt numb because he couldn't understand either how she could just turn her back on her family the way that she did. Secret was now 2 ½ years old and didn't know her mother. The bond between Lionel and Secret was tighter than tight. Lionel loved his kids and did whatever he had to do for them. He had no more friends that he hung with everything he did he did with his kids and Shayla.

Zuce had moved to Atlanta, Georgia with his girlfriend Nita. He was still hustling but had slowed down tremendously. Zuce and Lionel would talk on the phone at least once a week and Zuce would send Secret money at least once a month in which Lionel would put into Secret's very own personal bank account that he had for her.

Martina had turned for the worst. She had begun to drink heavily and all kinds of people had begun to hang in her house. Terri would go over there at least twice a week to check on her and had begun to worry about her because there was always a new man over there that Martina would introduce her to. Martina had lost so much weight and she began to look sick. Terri and Lionel had begun to care less and less about what Martina did with herself because it seemed the more that they showed that they cared the more that she didn't care about her own life. They began to show her tough love.

On the 5th of May was the day that Terri called Lionel with a phone call that she hated to make but had a feeling that this day would come. The police kicked in Martina's house and found lots of drugs including heroin, cocaine and crystal meth. There were 10 or more people in the house at the time and every one of them went to jail. Terri told Lionel that Martina needed him to come and bail her out of jail. Lionel thought about it and thought about it and decided to sleep on it. He let her stay down there overnight.

The next day after seeing Shayla and Mario off to their new home state of Georgia he agreed to meet Terri at her house so that they could go and bail Martina out of jail. Riding in Lionel's Lexus was Secret in the back seat and Terri in the passenger seat. Lionel had to stop by the bank to get the $2,500 that was needed to bail Martina out of jail. The closer that he got to the jail the more he wanted to turn back around and go back home. He had an uneasy feeling in his gut and didn't like it at all. He hadn't had any dealings with the law for the last 2 years or so. As they pulled into the parking lot of the Portsmouth City Jail, Terri went to the back seat to get Baby Secret out of her car seat and Lionel handed her the car keys. He begun to walk towards the building. Lionel walked into the building, Secrets eyes followed her dad with tears in her eyes.

"Auntie Tee is my daddy going to get Tina?

"Wow" Terri thought this little girl is smart.

"How did you know that Lil Mama?" Terri asked.

"Because the only time daddy cries is when he looks at Tina's picture and he was looking at it before we left" Secret replied innocently.

Tears formed in Terri's eyes as she thought about how sad it was that Secret didn't even know her mother. She knew Terri better than she did her own mother. Terri and Secret begun to walk into the jail, they saw the police handcuffing Lionel.

"Wait a minute why are they arresting him" Terrie thought to herself, not wanting to alarm Secret.

"Mr. Hayes we are arresting you because we have reason to believe that the drugs found in your apartment on Project Drive are yours. Being as if it was your house we have the right to tell you that you have the right to remain silent…

Blah… blah… blah...

That's all that Terri heard and the rest was Charlie Brown talk to her. WOMP WOMP WOMP WOMP…

"Terri look after Secret until I handle this." Lionel said with tears in his eyes.

"I love you daddy! I want my daddy!" Secret begun to yell.

Terri sat in the parking lot of the jail for about 30 minutes trying to calm Secret down and also to get herself together. Terri was heart broken, how was she supposed to explain this to his kids? Seeing Secret crying and so hurt by her mother's actions made Terri's hurt heart turn into anger!

Later on at Terri's townhouse sat Secret & Terri eating Pizza Hut and watching cartoons while Terri waited for Lionel's phone call. Ring Ring Ring "Hello!" Terri said expecting to hear the operator but instead she heard Martina saying "Terri I got that nigga! I got em!" "What are you talking about Tina?" Terri asked. "He got Marcus ass locked up and he's the reason that he's dead now so I can set his ass up. I got em girl." Terri was boiling and hung up on Martina without thinking about it.

"I can't fucking believe this bullshit this bitch has lost her fucking mind and has gotten Lionel caught up in her web of bullshit. She's out of fucking jail and got Lionel sitting in fucking jail."

Pacing back and forth on the concrete floors of Portsmouth City Jail was Lionel "D-Man" Hayes the street thug turned working father. He was in pure disbelief. He couldn't believe that the woman that he once loved got him in some shit like this.

"How in the fuck could I have hustled all these years without getting knocked for drug charges but as soon as I try to live my life right for my family is when I get caught up on some bogus ass drug charges? This hoe is dangerous."

D-Man called Terri to check up on her and Secret and could hear Secret in the background singing her ABC's. "Next time won't you singgggg with me."

"Hey Terri how are you holding up? D-Man asked.

"Well Secret cried for like 2 hours straight saying she wanted her daddy and all I could do was console her but then I said a prayer asking the Lord to please give me and Secret the strength to deal with the non-sense that's going on right now. As I was praying out loud I stopped for a minute only to see Secret kneeling down on her knees with her hands folded together deep in the prayer as well. Her lips were moving as if she was saying a prayer of her own." Terri fell silent for a moment while thinking of Secret.

D-Man smiled with pride thinking out loud.

44

"WOW, my baby girl is surely a soldier. It's been plenty of nights that I've thought my baby was asleep and I go into my room and just look over old pictures and just think back on the good times. I would end up in tears at the thought of my marriage just going sour then at my bedside comes my little girl telling me "daddy don't worry we're going to be ok." All I can think about as I look at her with big raindrop tears falling from my eyes was how strong and mature she was to be only 2 ½ years old."

A weird pause in the conversation. A smile came over Terri's face as she thought of Secret and just then Secret ran into the room while Terri was talking to Lionel and yells "Auntie Tee can you be my new mommy? As Lionel heard what his baby had just asked he begun to laugh because this wasn't the first time she had said that to him. As her and Lionel would play with the baby dolls and Secret would be the dolls mommy and her name would be Terri. She would say my name is Terri because I wish Auntie Tee was my mommy. As Lionel came back in from his thoughts he caught Terri telling Secret ask your daddy that question and handed the phone to Secret. "Hello daddy, I love you and I said a prayer for you today." Secret said and Lionel smiled and replied "I love you too baby girl and thank you for praying for your daddy Princess. Are you being good for your Auntie Terri?" "Yes daddy but can we call her mommy now?" She asked. "Baby girl if you feel that you want to call her mommy and she says that it's ok then you sure can Princess." Lionel said with a smile on his face. Secret said, "I love you daddy" and gave the phone back to her new claimed mommy.

"What did you tell her?" Terri asked and Lionel laughed "I told her that if that was how she felt and if you didn't mind then sure. How do you feel about it Tee?" She paused then in the background at Terri's house was the loud voice of Damion which was Terri's boyfriend of 5 years. Lionel really didn't care for Damion because of his rude demeanor. Lionel could tell that Terri wasn't completely happy but she was just settling less, but his heart went out for her cause Terri was a good woman and he wished that he had chosen her instead of Martina. Especially the way things had turned out.

"Terri what is all this shit in here on this floor there's pizza crust and chips on the floor. You know that I don't like to come home to a dirty ass house," says Damion sucking all of the life out of the atmosphere.

Damion bitched, and he made Terri's skin crawl. Just as Terri was about to snap back on him Secret ran in the room and tried to hug Damion but he just stood there and looked at her.

Secret looked at him with the biggest smile and said "Hey Uncle D (she couldn't pronounce Damion) my mommy Terri is going to take care of me."

She ran to embrace Terri with a smile Lionel sat in silence and listened to see how the situation would play out. Terri knew that all hell was about to break loose but she didn't care one way or another.

"Terri what is she talking about and why did she just call you Mommy? We're not taking care of any rug rats, not in my mother fuckin house we're not!" Damion barked in a harsh tone.

Secret stood there with a sad look on her face and she began to cry and say I want my daddy. Terri picked Secret up and held the phone to her ear with her shoulder and walked out of the room patting Secret on the back to console her.

"Terri are you ok baby?" Lionel asked.

The last word of Lionel's sentence rung in Terri's ear like a bell, "baby" thought Terri. She played that one word in her head for what seemed like a good 20 times. "Baby".

"Yes Lionel I'm ok. I'm just sick of his shit!" Terri spat.

At that time Secret was just as calm watching Scooby Doo on TV. She looked so at peace at the moment. Terri wanted only peace and happiness for this little angel because she deserved it.

Lionel then explained to her, "Listen to me Terri, I've saved his ass time and time again on the streets where niggas have been on his ass. Niggas was ready to kill that nigga for doing all kinds of shiesty shit like robbing niggas and then coming back on the block and chill with niggas like he hadn't done shit."

Terri could tell that he meant what he said because of the hostel tone in his voice. As Lionel finished his last sentence the operator comes through the line saying you have 1 minute remaining until this call ends.

"Baby call me right back." Terri pleaded.

Terri then realizing afterwards that she used the same term of endearment as Lionel did before. As she said that the phone hung up.

10 minutes later Terri paced the floor wondering what was taking Lionel so long to call back. 15 minutes later, you have a collect call from "D-Man" Lionel said. Do you wish to accept the charges? "Yes" she said. "Baby girl

are you and my Princess ok over there?" He asked. "Yes dear we're ok. Just wondering what was taking you so long to call me back." Terri replied with a smile in her voice. Lionel sat for a second with a grin on his face as the thought of the Terri being his woman crossed his mind.

"You know I was gonna call you back." Lionel said as he smiled at the receiver.

When Lionel said that he must have woke the dead because Damion walked in the room and started up again. Terri felt herself about to explode on Damion if he came off on her in the wrong manner. She paused to say a silent prayer because she felt a blow up coming.

Not caring of what he was saying, he started up. "You still got this rug rat in my crib and my crib is junky as hell! Girl you're one trifling…"

And before Damion could finish his disrespectful comment Terri stopped him and looked at Secret and saw that she was asleep. She wanted to make sure that Secret witnessed none of what she was about to bless Damion with.

She continued, "I don't know who the fuck you think you are and who the fuck you think that you're talking to cause I'm not one of these bitches out in the streets. As far as you and I are concerned, there is no more. You're a bitch and I can do bad all by myself. Please don't forget that I made you who the fuck you are. Yep, I made you the piece of shit that you are today, and I do mean piece of shit. You never deserved me anyways so my ass is what you can kiss cause IT'S OVER!"

Damion stood there with shock written all over his face and rage in his voice. He looked as if he had just saw a ghost. He didn't have a comeback so he had to think quickly.

"Fuck you Terri! You're not leaving me cause you have nowhere to go remember. Where the fuck you gonna go?" Damion thought that he had there.

"Don't worry about where I'm going. I'm no longer your concern." Terri responded.

She then turned to make sure that Secret was still asleep and saw that she was no longer in the room and started to immediately panic.

"Oh my God. Secret where are you?" Terri shouted as she forgot she was on the phone with Lionel.

"Terri what's wrong with Secret?" Lionel interjected.

Terri started running through the house and so was Damion. They searched the whole house but couldn't seem to find her. As Terri stood in a trance she started crying and dropped the telephone.

"Terri! Terri! Terri!" Lionel yelled louder and louder each time.

No response was given from Terri because she had dropped the phone and hadn't realized it. Secret sat quietly in the bathtub as she cried silently and prayed to herself. She would do this whenever she felt any type of tension in the room or anywhere around her. She sat there and prayed, Shayla taught her how to pray when she was a year old, although at first she could only say a few words but she had the concept down to a science. Shayla kept Secret in church every single Sunday faithfully as her mother did her.

Terri dropped the phone and her body dropped as well hitting the hardwood floors in tears. As the floor was the comfort that she needed at the moment because she had gotten weak all of a sudden. Her entire body fell limp at the thought of losing Secret or to see her hurt in any kind of way. In the middle of her sobs, she could hear a ringing in her ear and thought that maybe she had hit her head on the floor or something. Damion quickly bought her back to reality with the sound of his harsh voice.

"Are you gonna pick up that damn phone stupid or shall I?" Damion said as if he were making things any better.

Without hesitation she answered the phone to hear the operator's voice. "Yes operator I'll accept the call."

Lionel said in a worried tone. "Tee is everything ok? Where is Secret?"

Terri fell silent because she had no answers for this man's questions about where his child was. Tears filled up again as she tried to find the right thing to say but before she could say anything Damion walked back into the room again in an uproar.

"That little bastard is in the bathroom in the bath tub with her stupid ass."

Terri jumped up and before she could tell Lionel to hold on she hung up the phone without even thinking about what she had done. Reaching the bathroom and seeing Secret's innocent face looking so sad. Terri felt like a building, fuck a brick but a building had been lifted off of her shoulders. Terri reached her hands out for Secret to come to her but she just sat there and shook her head "No."

Tears flowed like a river and Terri could see the fear in Secret's eyes so Terri just climbed into the tub with her. Secret wiped away her tears but they continued to flow and told her to pray with her, and they did just that.

Chapter 6 A Phone Call That Could Cost Damion His Life

Terri and Secret continued to pray prayers of their own. Terri's prayer was asking the Lord to bless D-Man because she knew that he was innocent. Also for the Lord to bless Secret and to keep her the strong lil girl that she is and for her to grow into an even stronger young lady despite her rough childhood and all the drama with her parents. Terri lastly said a prayer for herself asking the Lord to remove her from her situation that she was in because she knew that it was an unhealthy one and she was very unhappy.

Secret's prayed. "God please bring my daddy home and God bless mommy Terri she loves me and I love her. Please bless Mario and Auntie Shayla."

But before Terri could finish ear hustling on Secret's prayers she could hear Damion's loud laugh and jumped up and told Secret to stay there and keep praying and she'll be right back.

As she walked into the kitchen where she could hear Damion now talking and suddenly shouting loudly.

"Nigga who the fuck do you think you are? You may be the man when you're out on these streets but you're behind those bars now so fuck you. Matter of fact, you need to find someone to come and get this lil bastard of a child of yours. Oh yeah Martina must have been getting high during her pregnancy because that lil bitch is slow as hell. She goes and sits in the bathtub while we're searching for her."

As Damion intended on keeping up the upper cuts to the gut while he tried to damage D-Man's ego. He didn't realize that he's only adding fuel to his own fire that D-Man already had filled within him.

Terri said, "How the fuck you know so much about what's going on with D-Man because I haven't told your bitch ass shit and if you ever disrespect Secret ever again I swear I will fuck your bitch ass up because you're nothing but a bitch! Why the fuck you wait until D-Man is in jail to wanna talk tough shit!? Because you're a bitch!" Terri yelled.

D-Man on the other end of the phone fuming and pacing the floor. "Oh bitch you done fucked up now, but just hold tight and see what the fuck I got coming to you. Just sit tight nigga." And just that quick D-Man hung up the phone.

"Why the fuck you hang up the fucking phone you bitch?" asked Terri. "How the fuck you know so much about D-Man and his case nigga?"

And Damion replied, "You're so called best friend or who you think is your best friend Martina keeps me informed on everything, she's my new bestie ha ha ha ha." Damion chuckled.

Terri sat with a blank look on her face as it was all becoming clearer to her, as she replayed several conversations in her head that Damion had started up with her. He knew too much of everybody information Terri thought. "Would Tina stoop that low to fuck with this no good ass nigga Damion behind my back? She got a great husband that's devoted and an excellent father to their kids and she chooses to betray him and me too, well payback is a motherfucker Martina Hayes."

Damion sat there taking D-Man's words lightly like he couldn't make things happen from behind those bars. Damion lit a blunt right there in the house which was something that they've always agreed to never smoke in the house and especially when they had company.

Terri went back into the bathroom with Secret to check on her and when she smelled the loud stench of purple haze fill the air. She got up and closed the door to the bathroom. Terri had planned on the two of them sleeping there because that was where Secret felt safe and that was all that Terri wanted for Secret. Terri laid there with Secret in her arms she sat and begun to think how she could make things right and what would be her next move because she had nowhere else to go. She didn't deal with her family, most of them were either dead, in jail, or on drugs or straight up shady and crazy as hell so that was definitely out of the question. Martina was simply also out of the question because she had some plans of get back for her. "Could I use that as part of my get back plan by staying with her? Naw I can't even stand to be in that bitches presence right now because I would probably kill her." Terri thought. In the middle of her thinking and brainstorming she dozed off into a light sleep and began dreaming of the perfect revenge.

Back at the Portsmouth City Jail, Lionel could not sit still from everything that was going on over the past 6 hours. He had made 2 phone calls and his problem was soon to be dealt with. He decided to call his son Mario and check on them and also fill him in on what was going on with them.

Zuce couldn't believe the non-sense that he had just heard from his best friend D-Man and couldn't believe that he was in jail at that. Zuce and Nita had just gotten to Portsmouth the day before because Nita had a hair show to do in 2 days. He was just thankful that he was there in Portsmouth right then and there to be there for his best friend, the man that's been there for everybody else when he was in the dope game and never asked anything of anybody.

As the car came to a halt, Zuce put his Newport out and said "Are you ready to handle business?" Zuce asked Scotty his brother-in-law who had been Zuce's right hand man since he had been in Atlanta. Scotty had heard so much about D-Man and had met him only once but realized a real man when he saw one. It was only a word when Zuce had told him what was up with this nigga Damion and the plans for his shawty Terri and Secret. "Yep, that's an understatement Zuce" said Scotty in a hyped tone. Zuce fucked with Scotty not only because he was Nita's brother but he was a real ass thorough ass nigga.

Soon as Zuce stepped onto the Atlanta scene, Scotty was the first dude that Zuce met. Zuce was at the barbershop on Buck Head called 'Cuttin Up' and Shawn the neighborhood bully (which he thought he was anyways) had tried to play Zuce because he knew Zuce wasn't from around there from his VA Fitted hat.

"Oh so you're the Zuce that the streets is hollering about?" asked Shawn in a sly tone.

Zuce sat with a puzzled look on his face because this was only his second time at this shop and only his second month in Atlanta. True he had a couple of connects in Atlanta even before he moved there but Zuce kept it low key.

Shawn looked at Zuce and said, "Why you looking at me like that nigga, so you're a VA cat huh? I heard VA is for lovers my nigga and that's some bitch shit, we don't have time for love round these parts. We're gangstas out here in the A nigga. Imma call you 'Lover Boy' my nigga." He laughed.

Zuce had enough of this bullshittin ass nigga trying to disrespect him and his home state. Zuce stood up ready to put a cap in this nigga's ass, Shawn saw the serious look on Zuce's face and got a lil scared. He tried to laugh it off but Zuce had enough of this nigga. Scotty had just finished with his client and was now ready to give Zuce his cut but first he had to deal with the bitch ass Shawn who was fucking with his customer. Before Zuce could lose his mind, Scotty saw Zuce about to reach for his piece so Scotty stepped in and told Zuce he could go ahead and sit in his chair and that he would handle it while he patted his waistline. That told Zuce he had it under control and that he was strapped too. Zuce decided to step to the side and see how the whole thing would play out before he would pull out on this bitch ass nigga. The other barbers knew that Scotty would do just what he said and handle it. Scotty was a good dude and he was the kind of person that wouldn't allow anyone that didn't bother people to be bothered with. He felt as if it was his duty to save the world the best way he knew how.

Shawn's fear became even more apparent by the second as Scotty approached him. There was no need for Scotty to reach for his piece because he knew that he was just all mouth but Scotty thought that it was time to shut this nigga up or make him show what he was all about.

"Yo nigga why you always talking shit, but nobody's ever seen you do shit? And you hollering bout round here we're gangsta's nigga. If you's a gangsta nigga then you don't have to talk about it cause you know what you're about. I love my hometown but I also know that it's the home of the gays as well my dude. You fit right in, no offense my niggas" he said as he began looking around at the rest of the ATL niggas, "but this nigga just feel like he can disrespect the next man and where they're from when he doesn't make his home state look good at all. What ever happened to southern hospitality homie? Matter of fact I love VA cause they got some of the most beautiful women I've ever seen. So fuck that shit you talking witcha homo ass" said Scotty in a laugh so loud the whole barbershop burst into laughter. Shawn sat ready to cry but couldn't allow himself to do so. "Now next time I won't be so nice with that ass so think twice before you wanna disrespect one of my clients" Scotty said walking away and proceeding to go and cut Zuce's hair.

Giving Zuce dap before putting the cape on him, Scotty looked at Zuce for a look of approval to see if Zuce had felt as if he had handled it and just then Zuce nodded at him.

"Thanks homie cause I was about to put dat nigga in Atlanta's finest, the hospital that is." Zuce gave a stern look to let Shawn know that he was serious.

They both laughed as Zuce realized that Scotty was a real dude and he knew that he could fuck with dude tough and not to mention he was one of the hottest barbers in the 'A.' Shawn sat with a silly look on his face for the rest of the day. Scotty and Zuce chopped it up and chatted for a while. They found that they had a whole lot in common. Zuce sat in the shop talking to Scotty & Rod another one of the barbers in the shop about sports. They were all New York Giants fans and loved the Yankees as well. Scotty told Zuce that he was having a birthday party for his sister Nita at Club 112 and wanted Zuce to come out and party with them.

Zuce started not to go because clubs just weren't his thing but he decided that he needed to get his social life up to par. Dressed in his all white linen suit and his fresh Air Force One's and a 5 carat gold pinky ring with the matching necklace and bracelet.

The night went well for the party and once Nita laid eyes on Zuce she knew she had to have him as her man. Nita was a very beautiful young lady that carried herself as a lady at all times. Standing at 5ft 4in with a behind the size of a watermelon. She had the body of a goddess and the face of a beauty queen and the personality to die for but she had low tolerance for men with a whole lot of bullshit with them. She wasn't too pressed on having a man until she laid eyes on Zuce. Zuce stood there talking to Scotty about their next business move that they were considering. Nita stood across the room admiring the dark skinned nice frame with the stance of a stallion and let me not forget those sexy bow legs. Not to mention he put her in the mind of her favorite actor Morris Chestnut, yummy she thought. Zuce noticed Nita eyeing him and he liked what he saw as well. He was so mesmerized by Nita's beauty because he felt like she looked like the actor Lisa Ray. He was so taken by her beauty that he heard nothing of what Scotty had said in the last 5 minutes of their convo.

"Hey Scott who is this beautiful dime over there in the all-white one piece?" asked Zuce with a serious look on his face.

Scotty turned and looked in the direction of Zuce's gaze and burst into laughter as he said "Who Nita? Shit man that's my everything right there." Zuce had an embarrassed look on his face and replied "Oh shit my nigga I apologize. I didn't know that was you my dude." Zuce looked real disappointed until Scotty said "Naw nigga that's not my shawty. That's my sister the lady of the hour. Come on my dude let me introduce you two."

Nita noticed her brother and the fine excuse of a man walking in her direction. She pretended not to notice and began fixing her lip gloss. As they got in the presence of Nita, Zuce felt as if she had taken his breath away and that she was the true definition of breathtaking. Zuce found himself at a loss for words and this was a first for him. Once they were formally introduced they were in a world of their own and Scotty left them to themselves.

For the next 3 months they were inseparable and didn't miss a lunch or a dinner date daily. They spent plenty of nights together but didn't once engage in sex because they were busy enjoying one another. From that day of the party it was a wrap. They were an item. Unlike most brother's that loved their sister and felt as if they were their sister's protector, Scotty on the other hand was happy just to see his sister happy and to make it better he really fucked with Zuce. Scotty felt that he was a good cat.

Zuce snapped out of his trip down memory lane about the past 3 years, he noticed the front door of Damion and Terri's house door opening and yelled "BINGO!" Scotty spotted Damion exiting the crib as though he was in a hurry. Scotty put the key in the ignition and pulled the Ford Mustang up behind Damion's Nissan Maxima so that he couldn't get out of the driveway. Damion had already seen the 2 men sitting in front of his 2 story town home for the last 15 minutes. Once he saw the driver door open he noticed that it was Zuce in the passenger seat. He knew that D-Man had sent him. Why he thought that he could get away was unknown to him. Where he thought he would go was unclear to him as well. He thought to himself "I just have to get out of here and then I'll figure out the rest later."

Scotty was the first to exit the whip leaving Zuce in the whip putting his piece in his waistband just in case he needed it even though D-Man had already made it clear not to body the clown. He was asked to just shake him up and let him know who he was fucking with. Damion sat in the car like a lil bitch with the windows rolled up and the doors locked. Scotty found this amusing but quickly got aggravated at the fact that he's not only a pussy for talking shit to his lady and disrespecting D-Man's princess but also because he's only a phone gangster.

"You got this nigga?" asked Zuce.

"Yeah bro go get Terri and Secret and I'll get this clown ass nigga." Scotty laughed.

Zuce started walking toward the front door, he turned to Damion who was locked up in the car like a bitch. He pulled the 9 millimeter out of his pants and pointed straight at the windshield because that was the only thing that was shielding his face that was now filled with sweat beads. Damion damn near jumped in the floor of the car and Zuce and Scotty laughed so hard at his scary punk ass. Zuce turned back around and by the time he went to knock on the front door Terri opened it before he had a chance to knock. She had a slight grin on her face because she had seen the whole thing looking out the window after she was awakened by Damion rushing out the front door. "Hey Z" as she would call him with a glad to see you look and a hug. Zuce could tell that Terri was either crying or asleep or maybe even both so he asked her where Secret was. "She's in the bathroom in the bath tub and won't come out" said Terri. "Yep that's her alright, and let me guess what she was doing, Praying huh?" Zuce smiled hard at the thought of his niece and continued "She's done that a couple of times before. When anyone argues or loud talks she would go to her safe haven in which is the tub." As they were inside the quiet but drama filled house Zuce asked Terri to lead him to the bathroom so he could see his niece, whom was his pride and joy. Secret knew who was coming to rescue her just by the smell of the cologne that lingered down the hallway. She knew this scent all too well. At 2 ½ years old she was often told that she had the strongest senses, they were out of this world and she had a memory for days as well. Zuce had on his signature cologne and Secret knew it all too well because she smelled it often when her Uncle Zuce would come to see her, he always wore that good smelling Joop!

"Uncle Zuce! Uncle Zuce!" Secret screamed jumping out of the tub and awaiting for him at the bathroom door to come and rescue her it felt like. In a sense he was. Zuce broke out into a slight jog as the bathroom was all the way at the end of the hallway. Zuce scooped his beautiful darling niece up into his arms and did his signature kisses for her. One on the forehead and then on both cheeks and she did the same with a tight hold onto his neck. Secret always had a way of making her Uncle Zuce feel good even if he was in Atlanta and was on the phone with D-Man. He always made sure he spoke with her if only to say 'I love you niece' and she would smile and say 'I love you uncle' and wet the phone up sending him a kiss through the phone and at the same time expecting one back in return. So no matter where he was he would return the same love to his heart and soul. He had no kids so to him Secret was the next best thing and she had his heart. D-Man wasn't his blood kin but was his closest thing to it. D-Man loved that Zuce and Terri showed Secret so much love and loved her as their own. He was thankful for them.

Secret wouldn't let go of Zuce and Terri was shocked at how A.) Secret knew who was entering the house and B.) How she had been trying to get Secret out of the bath tub for the past 2 hours and she wouldn't budge but as soon as Zuce came she came out.

"How did you know that was Uncle Zuce Secret?" asked Terri.

Zuce laughed because he had asked that question before and he was still shocked at the response she gave.

"I smelled him" she said sniffing his neck with a big hug.

"Wow!" Terri said in amazement.

"Well I do always wear my signature smell wells all the time" said Zuce as Secret still smelled his neck as he winked playfully at Terri.

He then turned to Terri and told her, "Go get your purse and any valuables cause this is no longer your home. Don't worry about your clothes and other things cause we'll get the movers to come and pack those things up and get them to VA."

With a look of confusion on her face she said, "But Z where am I going, this is my home."

He then laughed at her. "Oh Lord don't tell me I

gotta carry you outta here kicking and screaming too. D-Man wants you to go and stay at his crib for a while until he can get out and get you your own crib." Zuce said while shaking his head.

"Oh why didn't you just say that Z? I hate it here anyways" smiled Terri with a grin on her face similar to a big kid.

Terri grabbed a few things of hers and the little bit of things that Secret had there on the way out the door. Terri shut and locked the house up and looked at Damion sitting in his car like a little bitch. Terri laughed and said

"Hey Scott, what's good?" Terrie looked at Scotty and then smirked.

She then looked at Damion once more and hit the unlock button on her key ring to Damion's car and Scotty quickly grabbed the handle to open the driver's side door quickly.

"Good looking out T, cause your man had me playing the waiting game. I was seconds from blasting the door open."

They all burst into laughter at the sight of Damion squirming around the car like he's trying to run from his mother who was trying to meet his behind with a belt. Except instead of his mom and a belt there was Scotty with a 9 and his fist. "Let's take your car Terri." Zuce said.

"That's cool Z but what about Lionel's car?" Terri questioned as she pointed across the street at his best friend's car parked at an empty unit across the street.

"Oh word I didn't know his whip was here. Well

you drive your car and I'll follow you in D-Man's car boo." Zuce said.

Terri strapped Secret into the car seat that she had for her in her car she noticed Secret covering her ears and her eyes. Terri followed in the same direction of Secret's eyes between peeps. Damion's face was meeting Scotty's fist over and over again and Damion didn't even try to fight back. Zuce laughed as he started up D-Man's car and yelled across the street to Scotty "Meet me at the spot when you're done with this clown!"

Scotty looked and said, "Cool bro" and continued to hit him with blows. As Scotty turned his attention back to his human punching bag, the two vehicles pulled off and went off to their destination.

Arriving at Lionel's house felt like heaven for Terri. She had always had secret dreams of living there and her and Lionel being a couple. Terri decided to always keep this as just that a secret and never let anyone know of the fantasies in her mind of her and Lionel. How could she, she thought… This is my best friend's husband and I would never cross her like that or would I?

Chapter 7 Home Is Just Not A Home Without The One That You Love

Zuce entered the four digit security code into the home's ADT security system, he walked Terri through the steps of the alarm system as D-Man did him once they installed it but what Zuce didn't know was that D-Man had already walked Terri through it as well. She just stood there and listened as if she needed a refresher course. Once they got in and settled the house phone rang and Terri hadn't planned on answering it, just out of respect.

"Get the phone shawty!" Zuce shouted in a slight Atlanta accent.

Terri picked up the phone, Zuce carried Secret to the back and laid her in her bed since she had fallen asleep in the car after seeing the drama with Damion.

"Who was that on the phone shawty?" Zuce asked.

"That was Scotty he said he had been calling your jack but got no answer. He said that he's on his way and he got a story to tell" Terri laughed.

Zuce came walking down the hallway patting at his pants feeling for his cell phone. That wasn't like him to not have his jack on him.

"Oh I must have left it in the car, let me go get that before Nita calls and thinks that I'm doing something that I have no business doing."

He shook his head laughing. "That lady still has her guard up a little because she says that it feels too good to be true, and I keep telling her that it's her that I want and no one else. She's been hurt so much in the past that she expects the worse but hopes for the best and I can't say that I blame her. A lot of dudes these days take these good girls for granted and then when a real dude like me comes along I'm left to clean up his mess. T you've known me for a while so you know that I've never been the one to run women now have I?"

Terri looked at Zuce and smiled and had to admit to him. "Naw Z, I can honestly say that I've never seen or heard you talking disrespectfully about any women or messing with a whole lot of chicks and that's what I've always admired about you and Lionel. Even with all the money and all the street cred you must have women throwing themselves at yall but yall still remain gentlemen."

Zuce smiled and appeared to be in another world at the true statement that Terri had just brought to the table. They had plenty of chances to get at so many of these chicks out here in these streets and to be honest if it wasn't for D-Man, Zuce probably would have gotten caught up out there. D-Man always told him and his other homeboys "Everything that look good to ya ain't always good for ya." Boy was that the truth and plus Zuce knew that the playboy lifestyle wasn't for him because he watched his mother and aunts go through it and he refused to put any women through that. He lived by what I do to these women some man will do to my mother, sisters, aunts maybe even his daughters, so he remained a one woman man and if he felt that things weren't going good in any relationship he would end it but never without explanation to his mate.

Just then breaking each other out of their thoughts there was a knock on the door and also the phone started ringing. Terri went for the phone and Zuce went for the door. As Terri answered the phone she heard a voice that sounded familiar but in a low strained toned voice.

"Ha, oh yeah so you got your lil boyfriend to come over here and rescue you and fuck me up in the process huh, well it ain't over hoe." Damion said.

Terri started to get upset but decided that he wasn't worth it at all. Damion was miserable and she refused to lie in that bed of misery along with him.

"Look Damion, I had nothing to do with you pissing Lionel off. You did that yourself and I advised you to leave well enough alone while you're ahead."

He then started to scream, "Naw FUCK that! You think I'm gonna let you go just like that? After all that we've been through and all that I've done for you and then you send your little goons over here and to beat me up. Well I can't just let it go down like that. I know where you're at so I'm coming to get you dammit!" Damion aggressively said before he angrily hung up the phone.

Terri sat in a daze as Scotty and Zuce walked back into the cozy den where Terri sat. Scotty came in hyped up saying "Man you should have seen that nigga's face when my 9 met his face! That nigga literally shit on himself. Literally my nigga" Scotty chuckled. Scotty looked at Terri and saw that something was wrong and asked, "What's wrong T?" Zuce followed behind asking "Who was that on the phone Terri?" Terri struggled with the question in her mind if she should tell them about the phone call or not but she decided that she needed to tell them since it was a possibility that he may just be that crazy to show his ass up at Lionel's house. "That was Damion calling and he made threats of coming here to get me." Before she could finish Scotty cut her off saying "Don't worry T, we got you. I got you. I'll handle this nigga for real this time. I see this nigga don't appreciate when a nigga shows him mercy on his life." "Let me see your house key T so I can pay this bitch nigga a visit for the last time" Zuce said in a calm tone. Terri did as she was told because she knew that Damion wouldn't leave well enough alone and it would get worse off. She just hoped that he wouldn't wait until Zuce and Scotty left to try to get revenge on her so she had to do what she had to do in order to protect herself and Secret.

After handing Zuce the keys they headed for the door and Zuce told her to lock the door. He also advised her to take the remote for the alarm system with her throughout the house just in case Damion moved faster than them.

"Just hit the panic button in case you need to but I doubt if you do. D-Man got the remote for Martina for those times when he used to be out in them streets hard" Zuce said in a sincere tone.

Scotty paced the floor back and forth as he thought about all the ways that he could have blown off all this niggas limbs but he tried to take it easy on him. He had to make him pay. Scotty was a hell of a barber and well respected in 'The A' but by night he was a thoroughbred and wasn't at all mean but hated when weak people took advantage of good people. So he did what he had to in order to protect those around him.

Zuce went into the room to check on Secret before he left out of the house and he gave Terri $40 and told her to order them some take out for dinner for her and baby girl. Zuce started out the door when the phone rung once again and this time it was D-Man calling so Zuce went ahead and left as Terri accepted the call with a smile.

"Hey Terri I see that you've gotten to the house ok. Are you and Secret ok?" D-Man asked.

She replied, "Yeah we're ok D. Secret's asleep and Zuce and Scotty just left back out to pay Damion another visit because he called here and threatened me and said that he wasn't letting me leave him just like that. Also added that it wasn't over. He said that he was coming to get me back and some more stuff, so they went to deal with that." Terri said.

There was a brief pause in the conversation while they both thought about the things that transpired within the last 8 hours and after about a minute and a half Terri broke the silence and just put it all out there.

"Lionel the things that I'm about to say to you have been my feelings for a couple of years now so please don't stop me or else I might lose the courage to tell you. Please don't judge me because trust me I can't help the way that I feel. Now that I got that out of the way let me start by saying thanks for everything. Thanks for being a true friend even when my best friend wasn't. Thanks for being a great father and a hell of a man. Thank you for rescuing me at my time of need. You just don't know how miserable I've been living in that house with a monster. Only because I felt as if I had nowhere else to go and no one to turn to. I stopped loving Damion a long time ago but I stuck around for convenience. I felt as if I was stuck, but thanks to you I feel free as a bird. I've been in love with you ever since Martina started treating you wrong. I've always looked at you as a winner but just not for me. You were my best friend's winner. I knew that you had flaws when you were out there in the streets but even with your minor flaws you were the next best thing to perfect and it just hurt me to see you being taken advantage of. I was stuck in the middle of a rock and a hard place. I just decided to stay out of it but I always prayed for you to always be blessed in the situation. I felt so guilty so many days and nights about how I felt that you should have been with me and Secret should have been my daughter. Then I had to come to the realization that everything in life happens for a reason and that God certainly makes no mistakes. So I feel that you were with the right person that God intended you to be with but that never stopped me from loving you in my mind and in my heart. The way that I got the guilty feeling out of my mind and heart would be to think of how Martina treated you a long time ago. Thinking that you deserved better. I knew that one day the Lord would free you from the situation and I just prayed that we could remain close. Even though we became close because of my best friend's wrong doings, I still wanted us to be friends even if we could be nothing more. I love you just that much to just want you to be happy even if it couldn't be with me (she takes a deep breath and continues). I've been feeling a certain kinda way about you for a while now and just to hear your voice lights up my heart. Martina must be crazy to let such a good thing go. I… I…"

Terri became caught up for a moment and began to think to herself. "What the hell am I doing?"

Terri became quiet and shuts down until Lionel cuts off the awkward silence between the two and says..

"Terri I had no idea that you felt this way about me. Why are you just now saying something to me? Martina and I have been apart for almost 3 years now and instead of having dreams of me and my wife getting back together all I can think about is that her best friend should have been my wife. Terri I have loved you since the first day that I laid eyes on you. I wanted you when I first met the both of you at Tower Mall. It was you and Martina and Zuce and I. The only reason that I didn't get at you was because Zuce wanted you so bad but was too afraid of rejection. I couldn't get at you knowing that my man wanted you. So I guess you can say that I settled for the next best thing which was Martina. Which don't get me wrong we once had a beautiful life together and she blessed me with my princess but we weren't soulmates like I thought that we were. I tried to make the best of things because of the type of man that I am. Terri I have always felt that you were the one for me but I knew that even with Martina doing the things that she's done to us that you still were her devoted best friend. I had to put my desires of wanting you to the side and just pray on it. I knew that God would send you to me the way that we were supposed to be sooner or later and it would then be right. I love you Terri."

Silence filled the air again.

"Wow Lionel, so you mean to tell me that all of this time that you and Tina have been apart and you were by yourself. You were waiting for me?" Terri said with excitement. Tears begun to fill her eyes.

"Yep I didn't want another woman, not even my wife because if she could not only abandon me but her new born baby as well then she couldn't possibly hold the key to my heart any longer. If we couldn't weather the storm together than we definitely can't see the rainbow together. But you on the other hand have been there for me through it all and you still are and I Love you for that." Lionel said firmly.

"Awwww I love you too bae oops I mean Lionel."
Terri replied with a chuckle at herself because she really
did let that slip. D-Man let that go and didn't even say
anything because he knew that he finally had his queen
once and for all.

They talked on the phone for the remainder of the
night up until the deputy said 'lights out and the phones
shut down.' Lionel told her that as of today that was their
house and that she was going to sleep in the guest room
until Lionel told her to sleep in their bed under their sheets
and also told her to keep his side of the bed warm for him
until he got home. She loved all this talk about them. She
felt so at home there and was loving every minute of it. It
felt so natural to have Lionel in her life and she was willing
to do whatever it was that she had to do to be there for him.
She was going to start by getting revenge.

Terri thought about all the things that she had to do
in the morning starting with calling Lionel's boss for him.
She wanted to explain everything to him and was hoping
that he was understanding as Lionel said that he was and
willing to hold his job for him. She also had to get in
contact with his lawyer Susie Cuffee. She wanted to find
out what was going on with his case. Lionel gave her the
code to the safe and told her that she could use those funds
when necessary to handle the business of the house and to
take care of her and Secret. He said that Zuce had funds for
his Lawyer covered and that they would be coming back
and forth to check on them. He also told her not to worry
about him because he would be just fine. He said, "I have
faith in that because I've done too much good in my life to
not believe that the Lord has my back." Terri took a long
hot shower and washed her troubles, sadness, stress and all

of the worries of the past away. She was looking forward to living for the right now and the many joys of the beautiful memories that her, Lionel and Secret were to share in life.

After her relaxing shower she went into Secret's room and kissed her on the cheek, picked her up and brought her into the bedroom that her and Lionel would now share. Terri placed her on what would be her side of the bed and she laid on Lionel's side of the bed to do what he asked her to do. That was keep his side of the bed warm. Secret looked so at peace and content with being there with Terri by her side. In fact, she slept up under Terri the whole night and when Terri would get up to go to the bathroom so would Secret. Whenever Terri would move Secret would too. Terri had laid in bed with all kinds of thoughts floating through her head and then she finally drifted off to sleep.

Chapter 8 Over On Freedom Trail

       Freedom Trail was where Damion and Terri once lived together but now was his house without Terri in it. He didn't know how to act without her. He felt so empty without her there. In fact, all of those times that he wished that she was gone replayed in his head. He often called her lazy, trifling and nasty and in reality she was the complete opposite. Terri was a go getter by nature and worked hard for her money. She had only been with two men in her whole life and that was him and her high school sweetheart Ray. Her and Ray had known one another for plenty of years but had officially been together for 6 years and the only thing that separated the two of them was death. Ray loved Terri liked no one had ever loved her. He treated her like a true queen and you could tell that she was his everything. Terri had the biggest crush on Ray for many of years. He was a couple of years older than her and he was what every girl in school wanted. After she finally realized that Ray wasn't giving her the same love interest and she had chased him for a couple of years they ended up becoming very close but just friends. Eventually after she gave up her dreams of loving him was when he ended up falling for her because he realized that through it all she wasn't like these other girls. Her love for him was truly genuine and it took him a while to see it. Once he did, he promised himself to never take her love for granted and to never be without her again. They fell in love with one another and they were pretty much a perfect couple. They made a vow to one another to be there for one another through the thick and thin and to never let anyone come between them and it was working for them up until that tragic day.

Two weeks before their 7th year anniversary, he was in a fatal car crash coming from taking his brother to Charles City to see his girlfriend Nicole for the week and that's when he lost control of his Honda Prelude going around the curvy road a little too fast. He was talking on the phone to Terri so that she could keep him awake because he had just finished working 12 hours that day in the heat. She was the last one that he had talked to at his last moments of his life. He died instantly on impact and she took some years of her life to find peace within herself to deal with it. She never thought that she would ever love again. Even though after about 3 years went by she had finally decided to let someone in her heart but she never gave Damion all of her because she was still in love with Ray. She wondered if she would ever love anyone the way that she loved Ray ever again.

Damion thought about how Terri had come from nothing but had a vision of one day owning her own shop. The little black girl from Lincoln Park that grew up with nothing but had dreams of being her own boss and after high school she'd put herself through hair school. Then a year later she opened her very own shop called "Flawless from nothing to something." He smiled as he thought about all of the good times that they once shared together and then thought to himself "Oh I'll get her back," and that was when he called D-Man's house where he suspected her to be. He never meant for the conversation to go sour but just couldn't take the fact that she no longer needed him. And she was ok with not being with him. He was more hurt than anything and to get his mind off of it he decided to go to the sports bar just up the street called 'Big Daddy's.' He would have a couple of drinks to get his mind off of Terri and the fight he had with D-Man's friend.

"Let me get a double shot of the strongest Vodka

you have and make it top shelf!" Damion said to the bartender Kim.

She knew of Damion from coming into the bar frequently. Kim looked at Damion because this time he wasn't the same but she opted not to say anything about the change. She knew her job and that was to dish those drinks out and once they had enough drinks in them then they would tell everything.

After about an hour and a half of being in the bar and seven drinks later, he had filled Kim in on all of the unfortunate activities of his day. He was feeling quite nice off of the drinks and started to feel self-pity for himself.

Off in the pool room Damion heard a familiar voice talking very loudly and he thought out loud and said, 'Martina, what is she doing here?' "Kim let me get one more double shot please." After downing his drink, he walked to the pool room to see if this voice was the voice of Martina like he thought. He said to himself it has to be. I know my baby's voice. Martina was once his secret lover so he moved in quickly to see if it was her. Speaking loudly once he saw her, "Hey girl I knew that was you over here. How you been sexy?" As Damion stopped and stared at Martina with lust in his eyes she did the same and they shared a moment of stares while they're in their own moments of memories with one another.

Martina hadn't seen Damion in like 2 weeks since the day he had told her that they had to break it off with one another before either D-Man or Terri found out about the two of them. Martina had called Damion to fill him in on Lionel's trip to jail but he still chose not to see her up until he had been going through his issues behind D-Man on that day. They had been seeing one another on a regular basis and had been seen out in the streets together often and were both surprised that it hadn't gotten back yet. Truth is that Martina had fallen for Damion over a year ago and knew that he had fallen for her as well but only two things or people shall I say stood in the way of their happiness and that was D-Man and Terri.

Damion knew that he had a good thing and he also knew that he treated Terri like shit but he had planned to try to make it work with Terri because he knew that the only reason they had the problems that they had was because of him. He wouldn't allow himself to treat her like he knew that she deserved to be treated but it was because he truly wanted to be with Martina. He knew that D-Man would have a problem with that and also Terri would truly be hurt. So he told Martina that they had to break it off because he felt as if he owed Terri for being faithful to him and all that he's done was cause her heartache and pain. But little did Damion know he was in way too deep to even try to step to Terri like he needed to because even though he was at home more his mind and his heart was on Martina.

After about an hour of catching up and laughing and flirting a little more than needed Martina whispered into his ear, "Let's get out of here and go somewhere a little more quieter so we can be alone." Without hesitation Damion followed Martina's lead forgetting all about Terri. The two held each other up as they stumbled to Martina's car. Martina fumbled for her car keys as Damion attacked her and threw her up against the car. Passionately he let his tongue slide down her throat. She gave up no fight as she put her hand down his Levi jeans and fondled with his quickly arousing manhood. Not caring who saw them they both just let themselves go and do whatever they felt. "Oh my God Martina I have missed you so much. I can't do this anymore. I can't live without you and I refuse to." Damion said with what looked like tears in his eyes.

At that moment without thinking twice, Martina allowed her knees to slide down to the pavement as she began to caress Damion's full grown dick and balls with her overly moist tongue and throat canal. She began to deepthroat him right then and there in the parking lot. Damion loved every minute of it and his moan proved that to be true. Martina had begun to feel herself and wanted to do much more so she began to take off her clothes as she still kept Damion's dick in her mouth with no hands. The only thing that brought the two of them back to reality was the sounds of police sirens in their ears. Damion pulled Martina back up to her feet and began to fix her clothes as they realized that the sirens were headed across the street to the Gentlemen's Club. It appeared to be a fight that had broken out that caused all of the commotion.

Martina was now paranoid and unlocked her car door and told Damion to get in. Once Damion got into Martina's car without hesitation he told her to go to his house and she looked puzzled but decided to do what she was told.

Over on Freedom Trail Damion had just missed his date with destiny. Scotty and Zuce got tired of waiting on him and had just left from paying Damion a visit. Damion and Martina arrived to his house and began to kiss once again but this time Damion rushed her into the house. "Are you sure that this is ok?" Martina asked sounding nervous. Damion quickly replied, "Yeah Terri won't be coming back." At that moment nothing more was said about it by either of them. For the remainder of the morning they made love all over the house that once was Martina's best friend for years and her now out of the closet lover's domain. They made love in their bed, on their couch, in their shower, on their kitchen counter, and on their washing machine. Damion had Martina laid on the kitchen table with her clothes spread throughout the house. He had her pinned onto the table eating her as his breakfast, lunch and dinner.

The front door quietly opened. Damion was so into sucking the juices from her clitoris that he didn't even hear the door. Into the kitchen ran happily little Secret to make her usual fridge run to get one of her juices that Terri always kept for her. Terri thought that the coast was clear because she didn't see Damion's car and didn't take notice to Martina's car in the visitor's parking space. Secret stood in a trance at what she was seeing, Terri went throughout the house and saw no signs of Damion. Terri went into the kitchen to check on Secret before she went into the den to get what she had come there for.

She noticed Secret was just standing there looking sad and disgusted and Terri asked, "What's wrong Sweet Pea?" Then looked in the same direction as her and noticed the two mother fuckers that were once the closest to her on her kitchen table having each other for breakfast. Terri snapped out of her stares and starts to yell.

"Yall dirty dick bitches!"

Damion jumped once he noticed the confused look on Secret's face and the hurt look in Terri's eyes. Martina didn't budge as if she was on another planet from the things that Damion had just let Martina experience with his tongue. Before Terri realized it she had hauled off and punched Damion in the face and slapped Martina so hard that she had to have seen stars and possibly the moon.

"Come on Secret let's go home."

Terri said in a calm tone as they turned to walk to the front of the house. Terri stopped at the den and went into the closet and pulled out an old Gucci bag. The bag contained her stash from the last two hair shows that she helped produce and also took the prize home. $120,000 was the total of money that she had in the Gucci bags lining.

Damion and Martina still stood in the kitchen trying to realize and take in what had just happened. Once Damion told Martina what Secret, her only daughter had just witnessed Martina jumped up and ran to find something to put on her naked body. Terri moved towards the car in a rush.

"Secret honey, mommy loves you!" Martina yelled in a phony tone as she ran towards Terri's car.

Terri jumped into the driver's seat after she strapped Secret's seatbelt. Martina ran and started to bang on the driver's side window as Terri pulled off fast. Terri began to blast the music to try to drown Martina out of both of their thoughts and memories.

Later On That Evening

Lionel called the house phone shortly after Terri and Secret had gotten back from the park and from eating Secret's favorite which was chicken tenders and fries from the chicken joint called 'Fry Basket.' "Bae guess what happened today when Secret and I went to Damion's house to get the rest of my important things?" Terri asked. "What's that sweetness?" He said sounding eager to hear what she was about to say. Taking a deep breath before beginning to speak Terri started by saying "We only went there to get my money that I had stashed there and I didn't see Damion's car there so Secret went into the kitchen first to get a juice out of the fridge and when I went to check on her she was stopped in her tracks -sighs- Damion had Martina laid on the fucking kitchen table butt assed naked eating her out right there. They were so into it that they didn't even notice Secret standing there watching the whole thing. Tears now formed in her eyes as she continued. I'm not even mad that they were there together or about the things that they were doing because I didn't expect anything less from either of the two but damn I haven't even been gone 24 hours yet. "Baby let them be because they deserve each other. How is Secret? Lionel asked. "She's ok. She haven't even really spoken on it but she has been acting normal since then though." Terri answered. "Let me speak to our Princess." Lionel requested. Secret skipped out of her room to come and get the phone after Terri told her that her daddy was on the phone. She was in her room watching cartoons but was happy to talk to her daddy.

"Hello daddy. I miss you." Secret said with a big innocent grin on her face.

"Hey Princess, daddy misses you as well and I can't to get home to my two favorite girls. How have your day been and what did you do today?" Lionel asked waiting for Secret's response.

Lionel loved to hear Secret's little innocent voice.

"Well daddy today was long and kinda rough."

Secret announced sounding like she was more like 21 years old. "Guess what daddy, well I went to Damion's house today with my new mommy Terri and guess who I saw?" Not even waiting for Lionel to respond before she continued, "I saw my old mommy Tina laying on the kitchen table with no clothes on and Damion was sticking his tongue inside of Tina's vagina daddy. It was really nasty. I don't like them anymore because they made my mommy Terri angry and she cried daddy. I don't want Tina to be my mommy no more because she's nasty and evil." Secret began to sob and then handed Terri the phone and hugged her neck.

Chapter 9 God Works In Mysterious Ways

Lionel was furious from what Terri had just told him but on fire from hearing it from his baby girl's mouth. She shouldn't have ever witnessed such a thing. Lionel had to think of a plan to clear his name of all this foolishness that Martina had him tied into. He had to sleep on this one before he made a call too early that he would eventually regret.

November 12th

Secret was turning 3 years old today and had a big day ahead of her and she didn't even know it. Mario and Shayla had driven 8 hours to come home for their little sisters 3rd birthday. Shayla had baby London about a month early and she was now a month old and as beautiful as ever. This was the very first time that the family had seen baby London. Shayla gave birth to London on October 3rd at one of Atlanta's biggest and best hospitals Grady Memorial Hospital located in the heart of Downtown Atlanta.

It felt funny for Mario to come home and Terri was the one there at the house instead of Tina but he was cool with it. Mario had heard all about how Martina had been treating his father, and he didn't approve one bit. In Martina's eyes, Mario had turned on his father and was by her side 100% of the way. Mario and Terri was working together to get Lionel out of jail and Martina was their bait to make sure that happened.

The day started off for Secret in the nail shop where the mini diva that she was got a manicure as well as a pedicure right along with Shayla and Terri. Mario kept

London at the house while he waited for the crew to come and set up for Secrets 'Princess Candy Land' surprise birthday party. Everything was paid for courtesy of Terri and Mario. Secret soaked up the royal treatment as the Asian lady painted her nails and toes her two favorite colors of pink and purple. The colors also matched her Princess theme for the party. Secret knew nothing about the party and they were all anxious to see her reaction. As her nails dried Secret laid her back against the headrest of the miniature version of the pedicure chair that they had there especially for the little people. Terri treated Shayla to a pedicure as well and she looked to have enjoyed it. As Shayla shared pictures of London, Terri's phone began to ring. She hoped it was it was Lionel. Terri walked over to Secret and allowed her to take her first birthday call.

"Hello daddy!" Secret cheered.

"Hey Princess how are you feeling this morning now that you're 3?" Lionel asked waiting to hear her response.

Secret was so excited that she heard of nothing that Lionel had just said to her and she said with excitement. "Daddy, daddy do you know what today is?" He laughed and played along saying, "Ummm what is today Princess?" Secret whined and saying, "Daddyyyyy" with disappointment in her voice.

"Ok Princess, would it happen to be Happy Princess Day?"

Secret started to blush as if she had her very first crush and it was her daddy. "Thank you daddy you're the best and I wish you were here so I can be your Princess today daddy." He smiled and told her, "Well you're my

Princess everyday baby and daddy will be there soon. Real soon. We will have a 'Princess and Daddy Day' for your birthday all over again sweetness. I promise ok? "Ok daddy you want to talk to my mommy?" Lionel replied, "Yes baby let me talk to mommy and I'll call you back a little later to see how your birthday is going Princess."

Back at the house London was sound asleep. Mario was able to help the crew as they set up for the party. There was a red carpet set up for her and her guest to walk down and also a cameraman set up for everyone to take their pictures as they walked down the red carpet. There were life sized characters set to walk around the Candy Land. There were amazing balloons set up throughout the house in colorful Candy Land colors. There was a mini amusement park created in the backyard and colorful candy tables all around the house with candy bags with pictures of Secret on the outside of them that read Princess Secret. You would have thought that this was her sweet 16 instead of just 3 the way things were laid out for her. Terri thought that she deserved it because of all that she had been put through in her short 3 years of living. She was strong as ever to be a little girl. Terri wanted her to feel how special she was to so many people.

Being home, made Mario realize how much he really missed his family and how much of her Secret's life that he has been missing out on. He caught himself drifting into his thoughts of his mother and couldn't believe what she had done to their family. Especially his father whom was the man that did everything to make everyone happy. He gave Martina the world and served it to her on a silver platter and even through all the sacrifices that he made for his family she still didn't appreciate it.

Manicures and pedicures were done and they were

now on their way to Flawless Image Hair Salon to see Angie who was one of her close friends and master stylist that did her thing. Angie was able to work miracles and turn you into anything that you wanted to be. Angie looked at Secret and asked, "Is this the Princess here?" Secret stared at her fingernails and toes. The biggest smile came over Secret's face as she heard the word princess. Secret wasn't sure what they were there for but she was just a smiling. She loved all of the attention that she was getting for the day and that was Terri's aim.

Shayla noticed how Terri had seemed to be spaced out since she had gotten off the phone with Lionel and it bothered her. "Are you ok Mommy Terri?" She called Terri. Terri paused and then replied, "Naw Shay I have an uneasy feeling from when I talked to Lionel. He just didn't sound right to me and he told me that he wouldn't be able to call me from there anymore after tonight. I just don't know what's going on with him." Shayla interjected, "I'm sure he'll tell you more later on Mommy Terri. Just pray on it and let's work on making the rest of the day memorable for my little sister." Shayla finished sounding nonchalant.

Chapter 10 A Memorable Night Fit Just For A Princess

With a head full of bouncy curls and a sparkly tiara on her head Princess Secret paced back and forth with her wand in her hand excited about what was next. Shayla had picked out and purchased Secret her very own princess gown and she was looking as beautiful as ever! You could tell by the glow in Secret's eyes that she felt beautiful too.

As the pictures snapped Secret posed for each and every one of them and different poses at that. Terri made a mental note to find her some kind of modeling program to get her into. Secret yelled "Send my pictures to daddy so he can see how beautiful I look mommy!" Just as Secret got her sentence out Terri's phone rung and it was a long distance number but when she saw that it wasn't Lionel she didn't bother to answer.

The clock hit 5pm and it was time to get the party started. When Mario gave them the cue that it was ok for them to arrive because her guests had gotten there they headed home. Shayla and Terri were anxious to see her reaction. They had her blindfolded once they entered the driveway up until they got upstairs. Princess Secret took one last look in the mirror with a big priceless grin on her face she said, "Princess Secret is now ready ladies." Shayla and Terri burst out into laughter at her because she had so much personality even at 3 years old. Secret took small steps down the showcase of stairs with a smile planted on her face and her magical wand in her hand. She looked so amazed at all of the faces that she saw waiting on her to enter. Camera's flashing as the beautiful princess walked the red carpet. Several of her friends ran to the end of the carpet to greet her and they emerged in hugs. Terri stood with tears in her eyes as she looked all around the room. The parties set up came out even more beautiful than she could have ever imagined. Nita, Zuce's girlfriend had done a wonderful job with the party. She took Terri's small vision and turned it into a super beautiful Wonderland!

When you looked around the room you saw smiling faces, beautiful kids dressed for the occasion and what looked like a real live version of a 'Candy Land Wonderland' in person. As Terri and Shayla looked around the room they watched Secret take pictures with her big brother Mario. Then she took off and ran towards the two ladies and said, "Come on Mommy and sissy let's take a picture." Secret grabbed them both by the hand and then after about 5 minutes of pictures Nita told them to make their way outside and that was much more for them to see and experience.

They headed towards the backyard they noticed the mini amusement park and the many gifts that Secret had received. Secret had a mouth full of candy that she had picked up on the way outside from one of the servers at one of the many 'Candy Land' tables indoors. Secret saw Chyna her best friend from her class and took off running towards her. They got on every single ride there was out there until it was time to eat and cut the cake. There was so much food that it seemed impossible to run out. Her cake was simply gorgeous. It was a model of Secret's face with a Tiara on and it said 'Princess Secret.'

Mario helped her cut her cake while Shayla and Terri went over to the gift section to get the gifts lined up so that she could open up some of them. It was far too many of them to open them all right then and there so they only opened some of them. There was a huge box wrapped with a big pink bow at the very back of the table that Shayla insisted that was opened. Terri assumed that it was from Mario and Shayla. She just smiled.

After the kids played a lot more and ate, they decided to open some gifts before singing and cutting the cake. Secret got everything from clothes, money, toys and gift cards galore. Now it was time for everyone to come inside of the house for one last surprise. They entered the house for the final gift that they would open. The biggest of them all but Shayla insisted that the lights go dim. There was 2 tall chairs set up for Secret and Terri to sit in. As the two sat down Shayla reentered the room carrying a different cake with 3 candles lit on it and then out of nowhere they heard a familiar voice coming from the kitchen entrance singing, 'Happy Birthday' to Secret. With tears in their eyes Secret and Terri's dreams had come true just that quick. Out of nowhere Lionel had appeared looking better than ever. Carrying 3 little square boxes and so he handed one to Shayla, the next to Terri and the final one to Secret. He asked Secret to open hers first since it was her day and inside was a pair of diamond earrings. He told her, "Every real princess needs some diamonds." Next he hugged her so tight that Secret couldn't stop crying. Shayla was next. She opened her box and out fell a diamond necklace and he told her that she deserved that plus more for being the best daughter that any father could ask for. Then he reached inside his pocket and said, "I almost forgot my Mini Princess." Lionel turned to Mario who said, "Woooooo pops. I ain't no damn princess!" Mario had his hands in the air and everyone burst into laughter. Lionel reached his hand out to reach for Baby London and began to place a tiny diamond necklace around London's neck that said Princess on it. He kissed London on the forehead as she began to smile and he handed her to Shayla. He went straight to Terri who had tears streaming from her eyes just from the sight of her once before best friend's husband but now her very own lover in the flesh. Soon as he reached her he just broke down crying and which made everyone else cry. He finally pulled himself together and asked her to open her box. Inside was the most stunning diamond ring that she had ever had laid her eyes on. Terri started crying once again as he told her that this was just as a token of his appreciation for her holding him down while he was down. All everyone could do was cry as he told her that she was the true definition of a woman and he needed her on his team for a lifetime. Then he asked her would she be his wife once his divorce was finalized. Marcus McGhee is working on the divorce papers as we speak so it shouldn't be long that you'll officially be Mrs. Lionel Hayes. That's if you'll have me as your husband. All Terri could do was shake her head yes in excitement. Secret was in between both of them holding onto both of their legs. Lionel told Terri this is just a promise ring. That she would get the real one in due time. Finally, the family was together and Secret was extremely happy about it.

They went on with the party and after Secret opened the big box and she was in heaven! She had her very own Cadillac Escalade battery operated truck. Her and her friends spent the rest of the evening riding around the yard and the adults made their rounds showing D-Man some welcome home love.

Later on after the party got cleaned up, Mario and Shayla popped in a movie as London laid in Secret's arms asleep. Terri and Lionel laid in their bed and talked about their time apart and how Lionel managed to pull the arrival of his return home on his baby's birthday. "Cuffee worked hard to get me out on this special day. Actually I got released yesterday but didn't want to show up until today on baby girls birthday. Mario and Shayla knew the deal and Mario actually picked me up yesterday from jail and checked me into a hotel downtown and got me a fresh cut and bought me a new outfit to wear today. He even laced his old pops with a couple hundred dollars and that was how I got the gifts. I already had $2,500 on me from the money that I had the day that I was going to bail Martina out, ha but that didn't work out like that I saw. But anyways my son looked out for his old pops because I hadn't been to the bank. I didn't want to risk being seen by anyone and ruining the surprise" Lionel said. Terri sat there in thought and said, "But wait Lionel how did you call me from jail today if you got out yesterday?" Lionel laughed and rubbed his chin and said, "I got Rich from jail to call you from the 3 way to make it seem like I was still in jail." She shook her head and said, "So that's why you told me that you couldn't call me from there anymore?" Terri had a look of shock on her face and said, "Well never mind that I'm just glad that you're home.

They laid in the bed that the two of them would now share, on their sides face to face just staring in each other's eyes. Both in disbelief that this day of happiness was finally here for the both of them. It was their first encounter as a couple because they're normally on a brother/sister level. But not anymore they were now as one and they planned on enjoying every second of it. They kissed passionately and then heard some tiny footsteps and then entered Secret with sad eyes. "What's wrong Princess?" Lionel asked. Secret told them, "Y'all left me daddy. I wanna lay with yall too." "Come on up here and lay with me and mommy baby." Lionel responded. Soon after she climbed up there and laid on Lionel's right arm. Terri laid on the left arm and the three of them fell asleep until the next morning where they woke up to the smell of breakfast being cooked by Shayla.

They ate breakfast as a family and spent the day as one too. Bowling, movies, shopping and dinner was what their day consisted of. Lionel and Mario spent a lot of time together before the time was up for him and Shayla were to return to Georgia.

Lionel was proud of the man that his son had become. Terri and Shayla took Secret and London out just to catch up on lost times and Terri was happy to hear of the young lady, wife and mother that Shayla had grown to be. From the sound of things Mario had stepped up and became the real man that Shayla needed him to be and a great father as well. Terri had a chance to watch the two of them grow into responsible adults and at that moment Terri had started to get a little sad at the thought of them leaving. She had gotten used to them all being there together as a family.

Tuesday November 15th

Mario decided to go and see Martina before he had to go back the next day. Soon as he pulled up to her house he just sat there in the car and looked around at his surroundings. He was very familiar and comfortable out there in fact he kinda felt right at home because he used to hustle out there daily. In fact, he used to set up shop right out there. He sat and thought back on what God had brought him from, he smiled to himself because he had done some wild stuff and sold plenty of drugs but he was way happier now with his life than he had ever been. Sure when he was hustling he had more chicks than there were days of the week, and more money that he could count at times but now that he's experienced true love all the women in the world meant nothing to him if that true love wasn't attached to it. He heard people say that money was better when you earned it the honest way but he couldn't relate at first. Now he's seeing the bigger picture.

As he was in his thoughts he saw his mother's door swing open and out came Martina laughing and stumbling as she talked loudly and following behind her was a familiar face. He couldn't believe it, they really were a couple. Damion and Martina were high as hell off of something and just as soon as they stepped foot onto the sidewalk he could hear Damion being disrespectful.

"Bitch don't wear that lipstick no damn more looking like a whore. Why the hell do your clothes gotta be so damn tight?"

Mario couldn't believe his ears and thought to himself. "She left my daddy to let her best friend's boyfriend mistreat her." He shook his head in confusion. He was in his own world thinking how his mom had went from being the baddest bitch on these streets to being what now looked like a bum crack head looking chick. He snapped out of his trance by the motion of Damion's hand meeting Martina's face. He jumped out of the car and before he knew it he was all over Damion. All that you could see was Mario ramming his fist into Damion's body. Mario blacked out and started stomping Damion in his ribs with his Field Timberlands and Damion could do nothing but curl up into the fetal position. Martina ran over to Mario and slapped him in his face. She told him to get off of her man and Mario just snapped. Mario started cursing Martina out and that was something that he had never done before. He always showed her the utmost respect. But then he thought if she wasn't showing any respect for herself then why should he. Martina looked at Mario with anger in her eyes as she listened to the hurtful truth that he made her face. She had begun to mumble words that made no sense and was starting to confuse Mario because she wasn't herself. Mario sat there and looked at his mother with a puzzled look on his face. He noticed a young man walking up and saw that it was his old lil homie Shad that used to hustle for him. Shad asked Martina what was going on without even looking over at Mario and finally Shad turned his attention to Mario.

"Oh shit my dude, I didn't know that was you."

Shad dapped Mario up and then asked him, "Yo, do she owe you some money too my dude?" Mario shook his head and told him, "Naw my nigga this is my mom's yo." Shad had a look of confusion on his face because he knew Martina when she was every man's dream and now he's out here serving her. Looking at Martina her body looked used and saggy, compared to how she used to look.

Mario began to walk to his car as he realized that he had locked his keys in his car while it was running and his phone was in the car on the dash.
"FUUUUCCCCCKKKKKK!" He yelled. "Damnit man!" Shad walked over to see what was wrong and saw that he had locked his keys in his car. Mario hollered to Shad before he had gotten up on him and said, "Ayooo Shad let me use your jack for a minute to call wifey to get my spare key." Shad handed him the phone with ease.

Within 15 minutes the whole family had pulled up in Lionel's truck and Lionel hopped out as he saw Damion sitting on Martina's porch. Lionel had a look of rage written all over his face and Mario knew that look all too well. Not a look that he liked to see but when he did see it he knew that it meant trouble. Lionel slammed the truck door just as Terri was calling his name. By the time Damion noticed what was coming at him Lionel was already on his ass.

The only words you heard at first was Damion yelling, "Ahhhhhhhh Fuckkkkkkk mayne!"

At first no one did anything but then Terri jumped out of the truck and ran to Lionel. She said, "Ok bae that's enough he isn't even worth your time. Let that bastard go."

Mario watched as his father had torn Damion's bitch ass a new asshole. He had just got his ass spanked for the second time in one hour. Lionel began to calm down and snap out of his trance Martina stormed out the door looking like a true ghetto project crackhead. She looked as if she had a rough life when in fact she hadn't. The once classy young lady that wore the finer threads like DKNY, BEBE with bags and shoes to match now wore flip flops in the winter with dirty black feet and hand me down clothes. Her hair was broken off and damaged and the beauty that once was there was now replaced with a hard looking face. Terri nor Lionel could believe their eyes when they saw her. Before they realized it Martina had hauled off and stole on Terri in the face. The once calm tone that Terri once had with Lionel to calm him was now replaced with anger. Terri said, "You, fuckin crack head bitch that's yo ass!" She jumped on Martina's ass before she could get any words out. Martina was unable to land any of her punches instead she was fighting the air and every time she didn't connect her punches Terri would jab her again. She hit Martina until Mario this time decided to break it up. Damion spoke for the first time since Lionel had beat the breaks off of him and said, "D-Man you didn't have to do me like that. First your son and now you. So you know that yall are going to have to pay for this right? I was just fucking yo bitch you can have her back when I'm done with her." Before Lionel could react, Terri gave Damion a two piece hook to the face that made Damion see spots. They turned to leave and noticed Shayla standing outside the truck with her phone in her hand holding it up and Secret crying. They reached the car, Martina ran over to them and started cursing loudly.

"Both of you bitches are going to jail and imma make sure of that." "Come here baby girl. Come to mama." Martina looked at Secret as if she expected for her to come to her.

She turned to Secret with her arms open wide Secret looked away as she ran over to Terri and yelled, "Mommy I don't like her!" Secret hugged Terri's neck tightly.

"No the fuck you don't got my mutha fuckin daughter calling you mommy bitch! This aint none of your fuckin child!" Martina yelled as she went charging at Terri but before she knew it Shayla slapped the piss out of Martina. She slapped her so hard that her face turned. She turned to look at Shayla, she noticed that Mario now had Shayla's phone and was recording.

Mario started laughing and said, "I advise you to stop while you're ahead because we have everything right here and we will use it if we have to."

Martina shook her head as she turned to walk away with tears in her eyes.

8 Hours Later

Back at Lionel's house Shayla was in the kitchen cooking dinner for the family to get everyone's mind off of the day's events. She had Secret in there helping to prepare dinner and Secret was really enjoying it. Mario walked into the kitchen and told Shayla that her phone was ringing and Shayla asked him who it was and Mario read off the phone number to her. Shayla said that she didn't know who that was and told him to answer it for her. All Shayla heard was Mario say, "Yo who the fuck is this?" The male on the other end of the phone said, "Yo playboy just let me holla at Shayla." Mario slammed the phone shut and threw it at her and stormed out of the house.

Shayla yelled his name and tried to run after him but by the time she got outside Mario was speeding off. She called his phone back to back more than 20 times and he didn't answer. Shayla was pissed and ran back into the house and went to talk to Daddy Lionel but found him sleep on the couch with London on his chest asleep as well. She paced back and forth, until Secret came in there and asked was her brother ok. Shayla just broke down and hit the floor. Secret sat down on the floor with Shayla to console her by rubbing her back and saying to her "Sissy it's gonna be ok." Shayla could only smile because she knew that from such a little body that was some big words. With prayer the Lord would handle it all. Shayla said a low prayer. Secret still rubbed her back and Shayla's phone began to ring and without looking at the Caller ID she picked it up and the voice on the other end said, "What up Ma? I'm glad that I could finally speak to you without having to go thru your secretary. You got away from me one time and I refuse to let you get away again." Before he could say anything else Shayla cut him off by saying, "Yo who the fuck is this calling my phone and fucking disturbing my life!?" She waited for a response she heard a chuckle from the young man on the receiver, then he chuckled harder before he spoke again. He paused and then said, "You have no idea how long I have been looking for you. You just vanished away from me in the blink of an eye and today when that pussy asked me for my phone I just knew that I had hit the jackpot." Shayla got madder by the minute and said, "Yo who the fuck is this!?" She spoke so loud that she woke up Lionel and Terri. They came flying into the kitchen to see what was going on. Soon as they seen the look on Shayla's face they knew that it wasn't good. "Yo look ma chill out with the nasty tone. I'm just trying to reconnect with my old friend." He started to chuckle again so Shayla had enough and so she just disconnected the call.

"What is going on Shay?" Lionel asked.

Shayla ran everything back play by play to Lionel. Shayla tried to call Mario again and but still got no answer. After listening to the things that Shayla had to say about the conversation Lionel grabbed his keys and told them that he'd be back.

Lionel left and the ladies paced the floor for about 20 minutes. A little while after Lionel left Shayla's phone rang again with the same 802 number and Shayla nudged Terri and told her that it was the dude calling back and then the phone stopped ringing. It then rung again and Shayla answered it and put it on speaker phone and the dude said, "Shayla baby I don't know why you're acting like you don't remember what we had 3 summers ago." At that point Shayla was really completely lost. Just then Terri's phone rung and it was Lionel. Terri walked away and answered it. Lionel let Terri know that they knew who it was after talking to Mario and running everything down to him that Shayla had explained to Lionel. Just as Terri was about to say something to Shayla Mario beeped in and was calling Shayla. Shayla hung up on the unknown caller and clicked over to Mario and said, "Hello" in a frustrated tone. Mario immediately said, "Baby I apologize but I know who it is now. It's that bitch ass Shad. When he told you that I used his phone to call you that's how he got your number and that's how I figured it out. If he calls you back bae just don't answer it. I'm about to go and pay him a little visit right about now. What was the number that he called you from Shay so that I can figure out where he is? Shayla went through her phone and retrieved the number and read it off to him. Then London began to cry and Mario told Shayla not to worry about a thing because he was going to handle it and told her "Go check on my princess and I'll call back in a few to check on yall."

Shayla went to go and check on London but Terri and Secret had already beat her to it. Secret was sitting on the couch and had placed London in her lap and had begun to feed her. London was just as calm as she could be. Then after about 2 hours had passed and there was still no sign of Mario or Lionel, Terri and Shayla had begun to worry. They still decided to wait a little while longer to give them a chance to call them. While they waited Terri went into the kitchen and made both of them drinks to ease their minds, besides the kids had their baths and were now sound asleep.

On the other side of Portsmouth was like a totally different world from where Lionel and Terri lived. They lived in Churchland which was mostly whites but downtown Portsmouth was classified as the hood sections of Portsmouth. Lionel and Mario went to the bar called Shakers to figure out their next move. Mario called Shad from Lionel's cell phone because he figured that he would still have had his number from when he worked for him. He decided not to call from his phone. He called two times back to back and got no answer. He figured that little hungry penny and dime hustler would return the call to either chase money or pussy.

Many of nigga's went to Shakers to shoot dice or to

see the dancers strip. The father and son duo did neither of the two. They were at the back of the club playing pool with a pitcher of beer. Lionel's phone rang and it was the exact same number he was looking for. Lionel handed the phone to Mario and he answered it with a simple, "Yo!" To his surprise he got no response but instead he heard lots of talking in the background. He heard what sounded like Shad and another nigga in the background. Mario put it on speakerphone so that Lionel could hear as well.

From the background noise they could tell that they were in a club or bar as well. Shad had no idea that his phone had called Mario and Mario had been looking for him all along. Shad told the other dude that was with him that he had been trying to bag shorty for some years now but she was too stuck on that nigga Mario to see when a real nigga was trying to wife her. Then he went into saying how he almost had her a couple of years back when Mario was out in them streets. Shad claimed that Mario was out there fucking with this bitch named Trina from Chesapeake and got her knocked up. Shad ran and told Shayla because he felt as if that was the bait that he needed to make Shayla his wifey!

"Unfucking believable!" Mario shouted. "I'm looking for this nigga and he over there like some bitch discussing me like this shit is a talk show or some shit!"

Shad steady ran off at the mouth and not even knowing that everything that he was saying was being heard by the man himself. So he continued talking and Lionel recognized a familiar voice in the background say, "Shad you already know when it comes to us wanting these bitches we go and get em, no matter who bitch it is." Shad replied back, "Yep you already know Big Unc. That's how you bagged Tina huh? "BINGO!" Shouted Lionel. "Come on son I know where these bitch ass niggas is at."

Mario was driving and going about 70 miles per hour down the interstate and it took him 7 minutes to get to a spot that would normally take 15 minutes. Luckily the law was on his side and he didn't get stopped. Before they walked into the bar Lionel stopped Mario because he saw something in his son's eye's that he didn't like and that was death. He stopped Mario and told him that he had too much to lose to go in there and act off of emotions. Then Lionel pulled out his wallet and took out the family photo that Mario, London, Shayla and Secret took at the mall the day before. Lionel told him to think about all that he would be losing. I just don't want you to do anything that you will later regret." Lionel put the picture away and out of the bar came Shad and Damion and Mario's old running partner Nate. Nate walked straight over to Mario and dapped him up and gave him a hug of genuine love. Mario knew that Nate knew nothing that was about to go down but Damion and Shad had looks of fear on their faces.

Without second thought Nate said, "Damn yall nigga's look like yall just seen two ghosts." Then he laughed. Nate continued to fuck with them and said, "What's all that shit yall nigga's was just talking about these men here. Here they go since yall so real." Mario laughed because he remembered why he fucked with Nate because he was the realest nigga out there on the streets besides his Pops and Uncle Zuce.

"Yeah what was that shit you had to say to us my nigga?" Mario asked while Lionel just played the cut with his hand inside of his jacket pocket. And then the lies and stuttering began. At first it was "Man ain't nobody been talking about yall. What the fuck do we want to talk about y'all for?" Asked Damion. Lionel shot a look of disbelief at him saying, "Oh now yall nigga's wanna bitch up after all that shit that y'all was just talking." "That was that nigga Nate talking shit about you dawg. He was saying that he wanted your ole' lady and that he was gonna get her by any means necessary." Shad answered. And before we knew it Nate had pulled out his 9 and shot Shad in the stomach, not to kill him but to let him know that the disrespect wasn't to be tolerated. Without a second thought he turned his piece on Damion and told him that he would give him the same treatment but worse. Just like the bitch ass nigga that he was, he gave up everything and he sung like a bird. He told every single thing and even volunteered information that wasn't even asked.

Mario laughed because he knew that Damion was pussy but damn not that pussy.

"Chill Nate I already know what's real my nigga. I already heard these bitch ass nigga's talking about me and my pop's and my ole' lady and my mom's. I already knew that it wasn't you my nigga." Mario interjected.

Just as he said that statement to Nate, Shad grew some balls from somewhere and yelled in pain, "So what the fuck you come to do then bitch!" Before he could say anything else Nate pulled the trigger once more to finish him off with a head shot and turned to Damion. Nate hit him twice in the temple and said in a whispered, "I hate a disloyal mother fucker." Mario and Lionel stood with looks of disbelief and Nate broke the silence and said, "Mario you always had my back and made sure that I ate so you already know that I wasn't gonna let this shit go down like that." Nate dapped them up and just like that he left the scene.

Mario took Shad's phone out of his hand and just

like that they left the two men lying there on the cold concrete without a trace of them being there. They rode home in silence in their own thoughts. Before they gotten to the house they rode by the waterfront and Mario threw the phone and all of the drama of today into the water to rid himself of it all for good. Before they could get in the house Terri and Shayla was meeting them at the car and quite relieved to see them. Shayla told Mario she didn't care what happened she was just glad to have him back at home and safe at that. So just like that Mario left it alone.

The next morning, they were all awakened to banging on the front door. Terri jumped up and told Lionel that someone was knocking at the door. Before either of the two could get out of the bed they heard commotion. They both jumped up and ran towards the front room and was greeted by the face of Martina who was in an uproar. She was foaming at the mouth while yelling at Lionel "What did you do to him Lionel? I know you did it! Just like it's your fault that Marcus is dead! Everyone I love you take them away from me!"

With calmness and also concern in Lionel voice, he told her to calm down and speak to him. Martina then looked at him. She then looked at him real confused like. She stood there in a trance for at least 60 seconds, wiped her mouth and then said he's gone Lionel.

"Damion is gone." Terri said. She turned to Terri and with an evil look on her face. She screamed, "You're probably happy that he's gone. You bitch!" She spit dead Terri's face. It was obvious that Martina was confused because she kept going from high to low in a matter of seconds. Terri politely took Secret who was latched onto her leg tightly and walked her to the back den with a blank look on her face.

While Terri was gone Martina talked to Lionel calmly. She told him, "The word on the streets was that two out of town guys came to the bar to pay Rashad which was Shad's full name, a visit. The next thing you know they were found dead in front of the bar. Nate from South Side was at the bar and found them outside dead and called the police, but to me this just has your name written all over it. You're just jealous Lionel admit it, You're jealous because he had your wife and you want me back because that whore of a best friend of mine could never equal up to half of me."

Before she could say another word Terri walked up behind her and hit her in the head with her pistol without a second thought. Martina dropped to the floor that's how hard the impact was and Lionel looked at Terri with a surprised look on his face and asked her, "Where did that come from?" He said looking at the gun. She winked and said, "I bought it when you were locked up to protect Secret and I. Plus she spit in my face and that's the nastiest shit you can do to anyone. So I had to check her." Lionel chuckled because he thought that it was rather sexy to see the thuggish side of her, his ride or die chick. At that moment Martina started to move and rub the back of her head and Terri gripped the gun tighter in case she got up on some gangsta bitch type of shit. Surprisingly she didn't. She got up gritted on Terri a little bit and then continued talking as if nothing at all happened. Terri tucked the gun away when she saw that Martina had come to her senses a bit.

Once Martina was convinced that Lionel had nothing to do with it she apologized and left. Terri went into the den to check on Secret who was asleep. Secret was sleep before the commotion had begun. London was sound asleep in Secret's room as peaceful as she could be. Lionel went into the room and got his cell phone and called Mario. Mario and Shayla had gotten a hotel room for the night. Terri and Lionel wanted to give them a break from the baby for their last day there. Lionel and Mario laughed at the whole thing about how slick Nate had played the whole thing out and got away scot-free. That's why I had him on my team thought Mario. They shared a few more laughs and then got off the phone and went on about their way.

Chapter 11 It's Finally Final

  6 months later it was finally final. Martina and Lionel's divorce was final. On May 16th Lionel, Secret and Terri went to dinner to celebrate. Lionel had just picked Secret and Terri up from the shop once Terri was finished with her last head and they headed to Hampton to go and have a celebration dinner at Fisherman's Wharf. This was Secret's favorite restaurant of choice. They enjoyed their crab legs, shrimp scampi, fried shrimp, lobster tails, oysters and fish, and that's just to name the main courses. While they ate and listened to Secret talk about her day at school was. Terri watched as Lionel got up from the table and never once turn his attention from Secret and gave the head nod over to their waiter Tyrone. Tyrone removed the chair that was between Secret and Terri. Tyrone had left all of their eye sights walking away without saying a word. Terri was confused at what was going on and just then Tyrone reappeared with two of their favorites which was a banana split sitting on top of a fudge brownie but the one that he gave to Terri had a little pink box with a bow.

  Terri began to speak but Lionel hushed her up. He got down on one knee and told her that he had been waiting all of his life for someone that was for him. He thought that he had that at one time but he was wrong. Lionel would never regret the past. He looked at Secret and said, "Cause then I wouldn't have my princess." Secret turned and smiled as her daddy pinched her cheeks. But he also didn't realize that his everything was right there before his eyes the whole time. "Terri I want to know if you will be my everything, my forever, my future?" Lionel asked. Terri took his hand and told him that she had something to tell him as well but his answer is "YES." Terri then stood up and went and got her purse from the other chair and got a white piece of paper out of it. She then went back into her purse for an envelope and handed both items to Lionel. She asked him to open the piece of paper first and he did and was in tears at what he read. He jumped up and grabbed Terri and spun her around and Secret asked, "Well what did it say daddy?" with anxiousness in her voice. Lionel turned to Secret and picked her up to be on his eye level and told her that she was going to be a big sister and she yelled with excitement.

"Mommy's pregnant like Shayla was with London?"

They both shook their heads with tears in their eyes as Secret ran her hand over Terri's stomach and smiled.

"When is my baby coming?"

They both laughed and Terri told her, "Your Baby will be here in 6 months."

Secret was happy and then asked Lionel in a disappointed tone, "Daddy does this mean that I won't be your princess anymore?"

Lionel told her, "Baby you'll always be my princess."

They shared another family hug and got the waiter Tyrone to take a picture of them while he held Secret and had his hand on Terri's slightly pudgy belly. He felt as if his family was now complete.

Lionel went to sit down to drink some of his beer but Terri stopped him. She told him to open the envelope and he did and got the surprise of his life. It was an insurance check for $750,000. Terri had a life insurance policy out on Damion back when they were a couple. Terri took the policy out on him because of the lifestyle that he lived. Damion was a grimy street dude and she knew that his ways would catch up with him eventually and she was right. He was a good man to her at home in the beginning but soon found out from Lionel when he was with Martina all of the grime ball things that he had done to the niggas on the streets. Lionel had warned her that these cats wasn't playing with Damion anymore. That he couldn't keep saving his ass if he was gonna keep fucking over nigga's and that was when she went and got the life insurance policy. Terri never once said a word about what Lionel had told her. Lionel's mouth dropped in disbelief as he looked at the check and then back at Terri.

Life was good for them. Everyone was happy and Terri was due in another 2 months. Lionel and Terri was living a peaceful life and Terri even prayed for peace for Martina's life as well. The Lord listened to her cry.

On an early Sunday morning while Terri was helping Secret get ready for church. Lionel was dressed and waiting for his two ladies to get ready. He prepared oatmeal for breakfast and then he heard a low knock on the front door. The tap was so low that Lionel brushed it off as just as him hearing things. The knock got a little louder and Secret ran towards the door.

Lionel and Terri yelled in unison, "Don't you open that door!"

Secret laughed because she knew better but she just wanted to know who it was at the door.

Terri yelled, "I got it honey!" She opened the door and what she saw brought instant tears to her eyes, it was Martina.

Her once very best friend on their door stoop on her hands and knees with tears streaming from her face. The loving and forgiving instinct just kicked in naturally and she fell to her knees with Martina. Terri just held her and rocked and cried with her for an hour straight. Secret ran and got her daddy and he let them go through their moment together. Secret wouldn't leave Terri's side because all she could remember from Martina was bad and violent moments.

Lionel lifted the ladies up one by one and led them into the living room for them to get comfortable. He didn't want Terri to get hemorrhoids from sitting on the door stoop that was made of pure concrete. He was overprotective of his pregnant fiancé' and she thought that this was priceless to have a man adore you that much.

After about an hour and a half went by and the two women shared no words only tears. Lionel toted sleep Secret into the room with him so she could go back to sleep because it seemed as if they were going to miss church this Sunday.

Lionel was convinced that this was just another one of Martina's stunts to stir up some kind of drama in their lives. He let it roll for now because he knew that this was something that Terri had been praying on. He just rolled with the punches but made a mental note to speak to Terri on his thoughts later.

Martina said, "I'm sorry to come over your house like this T. I couldn't go one more day living with this bitterness or harboring negative energy towards the two of you. I've took a look back over my life and looked at every aspect of my life and I had to check myself at the things that I've looked back and realized about myself. Can you call Lionel out here so I can say a few things to him as well?"

Lionel was coming out of the kitchen when he heard Martina say his name. He went into the living room and sat across from them and Martina continued saying, "Lionel I just want to share some things with you and Terri that's been on my heart. First of all, I want to say that I am so sorry for any pain, anger or hurt that I've caused you. Lionel I also want to thank you for the man that you have been to me throughout my life. You've been better to me than I've ever deserved. It took for me to look back over my life to realize that you and Terri were the best things to ever happen to me. Lionel you have been nothing but good to me, outside of giving me everything a woman could ever dream of you also genuinely loved me and that's far more than I could thank you for. Terri thank you as well for standing by side when I needed you and also for loving me when I wasn't lovable at all. The one's that loved me unconditionally, I've let down. And the one's that's meant me no good I've loved unconditionally." Tears began to fill her eyes and everyone sat there in silence in their own thoughts until Martina pulled herself together enough to continue. "I've sat in my house for months to be exact since the day of Damion's funeral. It just took me back to Marcus' funeral and then the Lord was in my ear heavy. I have heard people say it but hadn't ever experienced it for myself. I've tried to ignore it but hey that man gets what he wants I see." She chuckled.

"Well what was the Lord saying to you?" Terri asked.

Martina answered, "Well he has his ways of getting our attention when he needs to T. Like I said, I had been going through my own feelings and emotions ever since Rashad and Damion had gotten killed. It was like they had become my only family. I was with those guys every single day and they looked after me. He made sure that I was good and at that time I thought that they were good for me. I now see that they weren't because Damion introduced me to cocaine and Rashad supplied me with it. I didn't need that nor those types of people in my life Terri. Where others would hate you despite of the wrong that I've done, they would really hate you knowing that I had a wonderful life and no one blew it but myself. But you were there to scoop it right up. I don't love you anymore. My husband, well my ex-husband is a great man and he deserves a great woman. That great woman is you T! I was wrong from the beginning when we both met Lionel. You spotted him first and had eyes on him but I made a move because I knew that you wouldn't Terri. Cause you're a ole' chicken." Martina said jokingly.

That comment brought a smile on each of their faces as they went back down memory lane for a bit.

"I've always knew that Lionel was too good for me." Martina added as she turned to face Lionel's direction. Her face saddened. "I knew it but I was too selfish to let him go because I didn't want him to feel an ounce of hurt and not a bit of pain. But not thinking that the things that I was doing behind his back was going to cause him just that if he had found out. Like I said, I've hurt the two of you deeply and I'm truly sorry. My poor baby has so many horrible thoughts of me because of the way that I presented myself in front of her." Martina sobbed at the thought of Secret's sad eyes looking into her soul. "I pray every night to the Lord to help me fix this if it's able to be fixed. I have faith in my God. I am asking that the two of you to try to please forgive me. Terri thank you sis for being the woman that I wasn't to my husband and the mother that I haven't been to my daughter. Thank you Lionel for being the man that you are no matter how much wrong that was ever done to you, you still loved me no matter what."

They all sat there with tears pouring from their sockets and Lionel got up and grabbed them all the box of Kleenex. He stood in front of Martina and pulled her up and told her "Thank you for being woman enough to sit before us and admit your faults and apologizing for everything. I want to thank you for that and not all of our moments were bad moments. Plus on top of that we had a beautiful daughter in the process. We ran our course and I hope that we can get past it and all and live life." Lionel looked at Martina and with the biggest Kool-Aid grin he gives Martina a hug and moves toward Terri.

"Thank you for setting me free so that I could learn to really love and feel true love again."

He grabbed Terri and kissed her on the lips and rubbed her belly. Just as he did he felt the baby kick and they laughed.

"So when is my niece or nephew gonna grace the earth to greet me?" Martina asked with pride.

Terri smiled because this was her old best friend talking and said, "Well you're nephew, will be here in 2 months." She looked at Lionel because she hadn't yet told him the sex of the baby. She wanted to surprise him. This was much of a surprise.

Lionel jumped up with joy at the fact of having

another little boy around the house. "Are yall hungry?" Lionel asked to the two ladies. While Terri and Martina were now embraced in a hug and enjoying the moment. When Lionel mentioned food they both said "Yes we're starving," in unison. Lionel laughed and said, "Ok let me go and wake up my princess and tell her about our football player and our lunch date."

Lionel went to the back to get Secret and Martina looked as though she got a little sad. "What's wrong Tiny?" Terri used to call Martina in concern.

Martina said, "Well I'm a little nervous about Secret not accepting me. I was already nervous about coming to either of you guys after all that I have put yall through but with Secret I'm really nervous." Martina explained.

"Well you don't have to worry about that Tiny. Secret will be just fine." Terri said with her purse in hand.

After about 10 minutes of Lionel explaining to Secret that they were all going out to lunch with Martina, Secret questioned why and Lionel put his best and fastest daddy forgives speech together. It must have worked because she finally stopped asking questions and put her dress on and grabbed her purse off of her dresser. Secret said "Daddy let's go and feed my baby brother." Like that they were gone out the door.

While Terri and Lionel rode in the front seat of Lionel's brand new Cadillac truck bought by Terri, Secret and Martina rode in the back. Martina picked up one of Secret's books up off of the back seat and asked Secret did she mind if she read her book and Secret said, "Sure why not." As Martina began to read the book silently because she noticed Secret looking her way. Secret said, "Ms. Martina do you mind reading to me too?" Martina began to smile and read book while Secret sat there and listened.

Lionel pulled up in front of Red Lobster, which was Terri's favorite spot since she was pregnant. "I haven't had Red Lobster in years." Martina admitted. Terri looked at her and said, "Well let's grub then." As they went inside and ate up until they were all stuffed. They all enjoyed their day and decided that they were tired but agreed to make Sunday's family day.

Before Martina pulled off in her Honda Accord she looked up in the sky because it felt as if a weight had been lifted off of her shoulders. She blushed at the thought of Secret hugging her and asking if she would come and see her, mommy and daddy tomorrow. Martina wasn't sure of how to answer it so she redirected the question back to Lionel and Terri and without hesitation Lionel said, "Sure Tina, if Princess Secret wants you to come and see us tomorrow I would hope that you would. From that day on they all worked on their relationship and became all quite close. Secret called Martina Aunt Tina after the first lunch date and Martina didn't argue with that, she was thankful to be a part of her life again. They enjoyed each and every moment together and Wednesday's had begun to be girl's day where Tina, Terri and Secret did girlie things like hair, nails and movies. Friday's was a day for Lionel and Terri to have a break so it was their date night while Tina and Secret hung out. People that knew their past didn't understand their relationship but neither of them cared because it worked for them.

Chapter 12 God Works In Mysterious Ways

July 2nd was a day that Terri woke up feeling great. Terri told Lionel that she was going to surprise Tina and take her shopping. Lionel thought that it was a great idea because he felt in a way that they kept Martina away from negativity and gave her the strength to stay away from the drug life that she was once a part of. He wanted so much more for Martina. He loved the direction that the relationship between Secret and Martina was going in. Even though Terri was a perfect mother for Secret but he also wanted Secret to know her roots. He didn't want to keep any part of her past from her but he would keep any harm from her. He felt that if she was into those things that she was once into it was his job as a father to protect Secret from it. Lionel told Secret that he was going to take her to the water park so that Terri and Tina could spend some time. Secret loved daddy time so that didn't bother her one bit. Secret went to search for her bathing suit and kissed Terri good-bye and it was just that easy.

Terri called Tina and told her to get dressed because she was on her way to get her and would be there in 15 minutes. In exactly 14 minutes Terri was pulling in front of Martina's door blowing the horn. You could tell that Martina tried her best to look her best but she just lost her mojo. Terri was there to help her get it back. Tina hopped in Terri's brand new Mercedes and threw on her shades to match Terri's cool. Tina was a very pretty lady but just needed a major makeover. For so many years Tina's beauty overshadowed Terri's but now that you see Tina in her not so put together days it was very apparent that Terri was always more beautiful than Martina any day of the week.

Terri was just the quiet as kept beauty and wasn't flashy. She had a smile of a model and the personality to die for. She wasn't the tight skimpy clothes type of girl. She didn't have to show off her body for her to be beautiful. For once in their lives Martina was actually jealous of Terri because she had it all. She had the life that Tina once had, the man, the money, the beauty and the life that any girl could dream of. Then to top it off she had her own money. Her own business and her business was booming too. She had just expanded her salon and had just opened another one in Williamsburg, VA that she had her friend Angie running. That one was doing twice as good as she thought that it was.

The first stop that they made was to Patrick Henry Mall in Newport News. She stopped at BCBG and bought Tina a whole new outfit with shoes included for her to wear for the day. Martina took the old clothes off quick and left out of the store high stepping. They went into every store that Terri knew that Martina liked and she left out the mall with at least 10 shopping bags with a new purse and three new pairs of shoes. She was very grateful for her friend and all that she was doing for her. She was starting to feel like her old self but just in a newer form.

Terri smiled as she looked over and her best friend had that old Martina glow on her face. Just to think she hadn't seen the half yet. They headed back towards the Newport News area and was going to Grand Furniture where she would refurnish Martina's whole house so that it would feel like a home again. Besides, Secret spent a lot of time over there now so she wanted her baby to feel comfortable while she was over there. Martina had no idea what they were there for but she was enjoying hanging out with her best friend, she really missed her dearly.

They walked through the furniture store and Terri asked her what she would decorate her house in if she had a chance to do her house over again. Terri told her that she was thinking about doing a makeover but didn't know where to begin. Martina had very classy and conservative taste and the things that she had chosen was very reasonable in price as well. The sales associate was following behind them and had already been put on to the plan so the young man knew exactly what to place a delivery for. Martina had done a great job picking out a house full of furniture for herself and had no idea as to what was going on. The furniture was due to be delivered the following day and Terri made plans for Lionel to be at Martina's house as the furniture people came to set up the fully furnished house without Martina even knowing it.

Later on that evening, Terri and Lionel went shopping for the rest of the accessories to put the finishing touches on the house. Secret was over Martina's house for dinner and a movie. Secret loved their time spent together and Martina felt as if she was slowly gaining the trust and love of her daughter back once again.

Martina called Terri anxious at around 10:30 pm to talk to her about finding the perfect building that she had found and with each ring she grew more and more excited. Terri's phone was in her purse so she had to dig for it. It took her a minute to answer it. As Terri was picking up the phone she could hear Martina on the other end saying, "Come on T pick up the phone for me."

Terri in a jolly tone answered and said, "Hey Tina what's up?"

Martina followed and said, "Sis do you remember when we were younger and said that we were going to open a daycare and a spa? Well… I've found the perfect location and building for both. The building for the spa is right across the street from it."

Terri was also excited at this point because she was thinking of a master plan to feed her folks and to keep the money flowing in if anything was to ever happen to either of them. Martina told Terri in an excited tone, "And it's right outside of the Coast Guard and Naval Base sis. You can't tell me that that doesn't have dollar signs all on it."

"Cool Tina. I tell you what, be ready tomorrow at 10am and I'm gonna have Lionel come over there and wait on the furniture people. I'm having something delivered to your house in the morning just to say thanks." Terri said in a sincere tone.

Martina got quiet for a minute and then told her, "Aw thanks Terri. You haven't changed not one bit when it comes to looking out for others. That's why you're going to be truly blessed."

"I'm already truly blessed." Terri sang and then laughed.

Terri gave Martina's house a full makeover. While Terri and Lionel were at the stores, they bought her comforter sets for her room and also for the other two rooms. They even decorated a room for Secret since she was now spending a lot of time there. Terri talked about the business plan that she had decided on. She wanted the three of them to open and run a family owned business together. Terri even decided to go with the daycare. Terri had already expanded her shop so she decided to go against the spa for the moment.

Lionel was now helping her run the shop. He helped her with the upkeep of the shop and since Terri had been in her later months of her pregnancy she had been in the shop less and less. Lionel went and cleaned the shop nightly and collected the money.

September 15th

The day of the grand opening event for 'Blessed By The Best Daycare and Learning Center.' For about two straight months, the three of them were hard at work with trying to get the bid on the building which wasn't hard to do because money talked. They managed to get the building business license and little work done to the building that needed to be done. They fully furnished the daycare, hired four extra teachers outside of the six teachers that were needed to run the classrooms.

When they decided to open the daycare they chose to make it a learning environment as well. Business was running smooth. The location was great so they had almost a full house at the time of the open house.

By the time the grand opening was coming to a close, Terri had to go into the office to take a seat because her feet were hurting. She had begun to feel pressure but took it lightly up until the pressure became too much to bare. She failed to mention it to Lionel or Martina.

Lionel and Tina cleaned up a little bit before the cleaning crew came in and then they decided to go have dinner to celebrate. Martina decided to go and get Secret while Lionel and Terri went on to the restaurant to get the table.

On the way to the restaurant Lionel noticed the uneasy look on Terri's face and asked her what was wrong with her. Before she could answer, she grabbed her belly and began to breathe heavily looking as tho she is in shock.

"Baby I think my water just broke."

When she finished her statement, she had another contraction. The second one was in another 3 minutes. Lionel made a detour to take Terri to Harborview Medical Center, where she continued to go into labor.

Chapter 13 8 Minutes And 8 Pushes Later

Martina made it to the hospital in record time with Secret riding shotgun. They joined Lionel and Terri in the birthing room. Lionel stood with a sense of pride in the middle of the floor with his brand new baby boy in his hands. The room fell quiet for what seemed like 10 minutes straight. Everyone just glared at the bright eyed curly haired little boy.

Secret looked as if she was in love and asked, "What's my baby's name?" Terri and Lionel looked at one another and smiled proudly and said, "Kingston Lamar Hayes." Secret smiled at the sound of her baby brother's name, "Kingston" she repeated time and time again for it to sync into her brain. "I love that name" Martina said with excitement in her voice.

Everyone took their turn loving on Sir Kingston while Terri got some much needed rest. Lionel called Mario and Shayla and told them the good news about the delivery of 7lb 8oz baby boy Kingston.

After they wrapped up their convo, Lionel promised to send him some pictures and then he had to make one more phone call and that was to his brother Zuce. Lionel wanted to let him in on the good news about the daycare and also on his new nephew. They talked for a good two hours while Secret and Martina snapped away at the pictures of the three of them while Terri continued to rest peacefully.

Life was great for all of them at this point, the daycare learning center was a packed house and the community seemed to love the business. They ran it with the most professionalism possible. Lionel and Martina ran the business without their business partner Terri while she stayed out on maternity leave for her 6 weeks with baby Kingston.

3 Years Later

Life went on as a happy and fulfilled life for about the next 3 years straight. Terri mainly ran her salon and spa and her business was very successful. Terri looked back on all of the people that said that she wouldn't go anywhere with the hair thing. She not only had all 15 chairs in the luxury style salon filled but she also had an ass load of clients that were nothing but loyal to her. The clients paid her very well for her services.

Lionel stayed busy these days with being daddy, keeping up with the upkeep of the salon and the daycare. He was offered a supervisor position in the shipyard and he decided to take the position. He brought Zuce in on the legal money side of the world to help out with the family owned business. They offered Zuce a pretty nice pay and benefits package. Zuce also had a company car and became the maintenance manager of both the salon and the daycare.

Martina ran the daycare and did a great job at it. You could tell that this was her passion. The four of them held a late night business meeting every Sunday night to get the in's and out's on the businesses. They worked as a team. Martina now had 3 year old Kingston in the learning center with her and 6 ½ year old Secret went to school.

3 years had passed and they had been so focused on their future and on their kids that they never took the time to make it officially official with their marriage. They

decided to finally make it official on August 7th. A small wedding of no more than 150 people, which could have easily been at least 500-600 people with all the people from their jobs alone. They decided to go against the big crowd but wanted to have a hell of a big reception to follow for those that didn't make the wedding list.

On August 5th Terri asked Uncle Zuce to bring Kingston up to the shop to her since she had to stay at the shop late to do two sew-in's. While she was doing her last two clients Ronnie her master barber at the shop would go ahead and cut Kingston's hair for her while she worked. Kingston had picture day at daycare on the next day and also the wedding was also in two days.

Kingston's hair would grow so fast. He had huge bouncy curls but Ronnie or Uncle Ron as Kingston would call him would cut it down and edge it up every week for them since the time that he was able to get his first haircut. Kingston thought that he was a little man hanging with the big boys at the shop as he would call it. He had the attitude, swagger and personality of a big boy and he loved being with the men. Kingston like his sister was very loved and well behaved so they had no problem with getting a babysitter if needed for their children. No matter where they were and who they were around their kids seemed to always be the life of the party.

11:27 pm, Terri had just finished up her last client and began to clean up her station. She cleaned up all of the excess hair that was on the floor. Terri gathered up the dirty towels so that she could get them together for Cynt her assistant to wash in the morning as she always did on Friday mornings. She sat at her station as Kim her last client left her with a $50 tip on top of her $150 sew-in price. Kim made her two week appointment for her restyle and pranced out the door with the confidence of a runway model. While Kingston and Ronnie sat in the lounge area playing the PlayStation, Terri sat at her station counting her day's wealth and counted up $855 with her heads alone. Then she counted another $2,250 for the booth rent from her 15 booth renters of $150 per week. As Terri stood to go put the money into the safe until tomorrow's bank deposit her phone rung and it was Lionel telling her that he had just picked Secret up from Jessica's house. Secret who had her hair braided up and styled for them for pictures tomorrow.

Lionel had begun to ask his soon to be official wife how her day went but she began to tell him how much the shop did today. They also went over a few more ideas that they thought about to include into the wedding reception. They got so wrapped up into the wedding talk because Lionel was just as excited and involved in the plans and planning as Terri that they had lost track of time.

Terri looked at her watch and realized the time, "Bae let me get up and put this money into the safe. Here king come and talk to daddy." Just then they all heard a loud boom coming from the front part of the shop. Before anyone knew what was happening a man with a black ski mask had Ronnie in the head lock with a glock to his temple. The man spoke words but Terri was in a trance. She couldn't think of nothing but the safety of her child. She grabbed Kingston who now had dropped his mom's cell phone in fear. Terri knew that she had to put her fears behind her and be the strength and the protector that Kingston needed her to be at that very moment. She thought about her soon to be husband and she wanted him at that very moment. She needed him then more than ever because she knew that he would never let anything happen to her or their children. Lionel wasn't nowhere around. Terri had to step up and put that fear to the side. Terri grabbed her baby for dear life and began to pray and run towards her office where she could try to lock her and her baby boy away into safety. She cradled her son in her arms and ran. She felt her legs give out as she had fallen to the ground in slow motion on top of Kingston as he yelled out one last cry for his daddy who was his hero. Lionel still on the line of the cellphone that was lying on the floor had begun to holler once he heard the commotion in the background.

Lionel grabbed his work cell phone with the left hand and called 911 and drove. He held his personal phone with the right hand. He heard numerous gunshots and the last one was the shot that he was assuming that was towards Ronnie. After the man that had invaded the shop had asked Ronnie to empty his pockets Lionel could hear a lot of things being thrown around but couldn't tell what was going on in the there. He no longer heard anything from Terri nor Kingston but he was still hopeful that his family was holding on for him. Lionel had tears streaming from his face and he could barely see the road but he was determined to get there to save his loved ones.

Lionel swerved in what little traffic that there was on the road. He never once thought about Secret being in the backseat. He had his mind on getting there in time enough to be the protector that he always promised that he would be. He began to feel himself getting faint simply from the anxiety and thought of any harm being directed at his family. He heard one last shot and then the cries of what sounded like Ronnie crying out for his life and then everything started to go in and out for Lionel. He wasn't sure what was happening to him. All he could see was visions of beautiful white clouds and pearly white gates and also pictures flashed into his mind of Terri, and then his guardian angel his baby girl Promise, his Princess Secret, his oldest boy Mario and Shayla, his beautiful grandbaby London and the little boy that looked up to him, his baby boy Kingston's. Bright eyes flashed in front of him and then everything faded to black…

COMING SOON
BY
ANITRA HILL

LOVE SLAVE

THE GAME CHOSE ME

SNEAK PEEK AT LOVE SLAVE

Dear little black book...

She sat there with lust in her eyes as her bare breast were exposed. Nothing on but her fishnets and black thongs which were sitting dead in the crack of her honey suckled ass. My shiny handcuffs binding her wrist together. I have once again sucked her soul out of her body through her cream filled pussy until she begged me to stop. I then pulled out my crooked piece of steel from out of my boxer hole and allowed her to watch me as I stroked my dick for dear life. She began to moan. This was the moment that she begged me to let all of my semen splatter all over her flawless face for her nightly facial... She opened her mouth with the attempt to catch every single drop. And people wondered why I was so in love with this filthy fucking whore... Asia Monroe was my dirty little secret, my own personal love slave... (Until next time)

I allowed my pen to drop. I thought back over my session tonight with one of my sex angels. She became one of my sex slaves and I must say that I was quite impressed at myself with my performance.

Raven, which was my wife had given me this little black book so that I could keep my memorable moments in. Now at first I thought that this had to be some bitch ass shit. Me, Zavier keep a fucking journal, (haahh) you have to be shitting me, but damn this thing might surely come in handy one of these days.

I had to admit that I did have a deep love for sex with women with clean, tight and wet ass gushy pussy! Me personally, I find it rather hard to turn down certain beautiful women with that wet wet. Matter of fact, there is nothing better than some 'loyal pussy' but some 'new loyal pussy!' I took pride in owning each piece of pussy that I fell up in more than once. I mean, I'm a man with a weakness and this weakness is hard to shake. (shakes head and then grins)

ALSO FROM KENERLY PRESENTS

Gotta Be Shiesty by Terrie L. Branch

The Streets Call Me Treasure by
Shaunta Kenerly

Like Mother Like Trick by Dannaye
Carter

Sweatin by Miss Kim

THANK YOU

Kenerly Presents wants to thank you for your purchase and continued support. We appreciate your business and hope to see you soon at the various book events around the country. We challenge our authors to give you nothing but the best in literature. Please don't hesitate to leave a review for this title and give us any feedback on our website.

Please visit us at www.kenerlypresents.com for more titles, new releases and updates about events near you.

Shaunta Kenerly
Mr. Paperback

ABOUT THE AUTHOR

Anitra Hill is a native of Hampton, VA. Writing is her passion and her therapy that she wishes to share with the world. She has a writing goal of giving her readers a much needed escape from everyday reality. Anitra has a library of titles soon to be released including the highly anticipated novel "Love Slave" and "The Right One At The Wrong Time" which is a wild page turner. Speaking of wild, "Love Slave" will have you clenching the sheets and begging for more.